SAN ANTONIO
 BEER

ALAMO CITY HISTORY
BY THE PINT

Jeremy Banas & Travis E. Poling

AMERICAN PALATE

Published by American Palate
A Division of The History Press
Charleston, SC
www.historypress.net

Cover images: Crowd photo by Jeremy Karney; truck photo courtesy of University of Texas–
San Antonio Institute of Texan Cultures

First published 2015

Manufactured in the United States

ISBN 978.1.46711.878.1

Library of Congress Control Number: 2015951457

FROM JEREMY BANAS:

To my boys, Quinn, Jack and Max: I couldn't have completed this book without you. You make me who I am. To my parents, Cathy and Milton Banas: I really couldn't have asked for more loving and supportive parents. To my sister, Cari Gordonne: To say you inspire me is an understatement. I love you.

FROM TRAVIS E. POLING:

To Margaret, without whose endless support nary a word would be written or a room brightened these last twenty-five years of marriage. And to my family—most especially my parents, Michael and Emily—for listening to me prattle on about every project and for somehow building an incredible office and library around me during the writing of this book.

Contents

Foreword

In 1918, just before Prohibition, there were five breweries in San Antonio. In 1990, just before I came of drinking age, there were two. In the fifty-seven years after the repeal of Prohibition, we mustered a meager two breweries in San Antonio. In my eagerness to try every beer I could get my hands on at twenty-one, I must say that neither of the flagship beers produced by these breweries stood out in the sea of pale lagers I found back then. In fact, I was convinced that beer was homogenous—that beer could be used as a descriptor for the flavor of beer. "What did that beer taste like?" "Well, it tasted like beer." Beery beer.

Three years later, the State of Texas made it legal for a restaurant to brew beer and sell it on premises to the final consumer. The brewpub legislation was the first ray of light to pierce the darkness of the Texas beer scene. Seeds that had been sown in stalwart pubs and bars around town began to sprout with possibility. Joey's on North St. Mary's Street began to brew its own beer on two small homebrew rigs in an upstairs hideout. The Broadway Boardwalk and Bistro followed suit with a small kettle and a bunch of carboys of its own. Both breweries were brewing English pale ales, porters and stouts—they gave us beer styles we hadn't seen produced in the state for most of a century.

Several more breweries opened in SA in the ensuing years. Joey opened Blue Star Brewing Company, the Lab opened at the old Alamo Cement laboratory by the Alamo Quarry and Frio and Yellow Rose Brewing Company opened in the mid-'90s. San Antonio had a burgeoning beer scene again. People were excited about beer, and the education of people's palates began. Beer showed its true colors—much more than a lifeless lager in a suitcase full of cans.

Of course, the bubble burst at the close of the century. Breweries went out of business for a variety of reasons: lack of capital, bad location or lack of a business plan. But people's palates had been adjusted—we were thirsty for variety and authenticity in our beer. The fuse was lit, and breweries would return soon with a bang.

Beer is like the hearth in ancient times—it's what we gather around for community and to share stories, victories and sorrows. There are a thousand and one beers in the nearest beer store, but we still seek to convene around a few pints at our favorite local. Buoyed by the boom in breweries, these little locals have exploded in recent years, and now it's no longer difficult to find a pint of beer brewed within a few miles of the doorstep. Cheers to that!

I'm very excited to have this new history of San Antonio Brewing from my friends Jeremy and Travis. With it we delve deeper into the rich brewing traditions of our city. We can follow along where we've been and cast our eyes ahead to exciting vistas we're still exploring. *Salud a todos*, San Antonio!

Jason Davis

Jason Davis is director of brewing operations for San Antonio's Freetail Brewing Company. He has worked at three San Antonio breweries and two in Austin since he started brewing professionally in 1996.

Acknowledgements

FROM JEREMY BANAS:

To everyone who has been there throughout the years for us, supporting every article, story, event, San Antonio Beer Week meeting, lecture and beer dinner that we've been involved in, especially the writing of this book. Among the many are Brian Orosco; Mark McDavid; Eric Cruzan; Keith and Zahra Cruzan; Art Cancino; Jason and Erika Gonzales; Jason Davis; Alicia Spence; T.J. Miller; Dennis Rylander; Holland Lawrence; Jason Ard; Paul Ford; William Les Locke; Jeff Balfour; J.C. Norris; Phillipe Place; Alex Rattray; Joey Villarreal; Scott Graham; Richard and Marie Mauro and the entire Mauro clan; Randi Jane Mauro; Julia Herz; the website bitchbeer.org; Ray Mitteldorf; Rob Garza; Nan Palmero; Anna and Keith Kilker; Kelly Meyer; Fred Hernandez; Bexar Brewers; Markus Haas; Seth Weatherly; Roy Wahne; Ernesto Malacara; San Antonio Girls Pint Out; April and Alfred Acevedo; Rob Martindale; Jason Armstrong; David Strain; Jaime Jurado; Meagan Parisi; Donna Norris; Carla Bowers; Robert Johnson; Whit Honea; Kim Krieg; Eugene Simor; James Hudec; Zac Harris; Jeremy Karney; Denise Aguirre; Ron Haluzan; James and Katie Vaello; Chris George; Sameer and Meagan Siddiqui; Aug Aranda; Daughters of the Republic of Texas; Carlos Cortez of the Institute of Texan Cultures; our fantastically patient commissioning editor, Christen Thompson; Neil Butler; Henry Halff; Brandon and Kim Hollas; my oldest friend, Clinton Buck Davis; the fine folks at Nebraska Brewing Company; Nicole George; Michelle Fedorka;

ACKNOWLEDGEMENTS

Michael Hood for his mentoring; Judy Gonzalez Hanley and the good folks at La Taza Coffee House; Sabine Weyermann of Weyermann Malt; Brooke Barker, whose unwavering love, support and encouragement kept me going; and Uncle Rich, whose passion for wine and educating others through his writings over the years inspired me to first pick up the pen all those years ago.

FROM TRAVIS E. POLING:

Besides respectful acknowledgement of many of those already mentioned by Jeremy, I also would like to recognize the assistance and support of New Braunfels historian extraordinaire Everett Fey; Beverly Wigley of the Sophienburg Museum and Archives; Carol Stein; the Bradburys; Scott and Sheena Bellavance Metzger; Allison Smith; Nan Palmero; Paul Hightower; Glenn and Cheri Whitacre; and the good folks at the Twig and the Pearl. Karen Haram, thank you for setting me on fire for writing about beer nearly twenty years ago and then fanning the flames. To the numerous beertenders who let me bounce ideas off them and drape my laptop-charging cord over their bars for free electricity, I thank you. To my mother-in-law, Felicitas Vega, for allowing me to take over her entire dining room table with research on every visit. Also, a special shout-out to Christen Thompson for her vigilance, patience and constant enthusiasm as commissioning editor for The History Press on this project and to production editor Ryan Finn for his eagle eye.

Introduction

History has always played a major role in brewing movements throughout the country. The first wave of craft beers in most cities, as it was in San Antonio, was a nod to the classic styles historically brewed in Europe. Ales, being the quickest to brew, saw a resurgence in American brewing, with the earliest microbreweries and brewpubs creating English-inspired pale ales, goldens or blondes, browns, the ambiguous ambers, reds, stouts and the occasional ambitious shot at Belgian styles. History was always invoked by the earliest brewers in the rediscovery of beer in the 1980s and 1990s.

As the movement began to mature, brewers from San Antonio to Milwaukee looked to their German roots of brewing. This often included a healthy dose of Czech, Austrian and even Polish roots for lager beers that once permeated most of Texas before Prohibition. Because of the longer fermentation times of lagers, however, most breweries in the 1990s and first decade of the twenty-first century were making them sparingly. It wasn't until the second decade of the millennia that San Antonio's own rich, pre-Prohibition brewing history truly became part of the new brewers' vernacular and part of the public consciousness.

In the earliest days of San Antonio's recorded history, it was the influence of Spanish missionaries that affected the alcohol culture. Alfred Rodriguez, Spanish archivist to the Bexar County Clerk's Office, noted that early documents mention wine inventories at the missions. A 1774 tax certificate for *aguardiente* (liquor) and wine was transported from Laredo to the Spanish Presidio de Bexar. He also posits that there could have been some cultivation of grapes within irrigation distance of the San Antonio River that could have found their way into native wines. Beer was not a part of the picture, although fermented cactus pulque and a naturally fermented drink of corn called chicha (a beer in which the enzymes in the corn are activated by humans chewing the corn) could have been part of the alcoholic beverage mix in the early days of San Antonio settlement.

Beer also wasn't on the menu when it came to relieving the tensions of the 1836 Mexican siege of the Alamo. Santa Anna probably had access to a few bottles of wine, and the Tennessee and Kentucky natives who made up much of the ill-fated party of Alamo defenders could have had some form of whiskey stashed away. But it wasn't until the years after 1845, when German, Austrian and Czech immigration to Texas began, that beer became a popular lubricant of the populace in San Antonio, New Braunfels, Fredericksburg and many other south-central Texas settlements.

As these immigrants came into Texas, so, too, did the thirst for the ales and lagers of their homelands. Just as water was integral to these early settlers and missions in the San Antonio area, water, especially the San Antonio River and various underground water sources, was integral to brewing beer.

In New Braunfels, San Antonio and Castroville between 1851 and 1870, numerous breweries of various sizes popped up. Some would fail but would inspire others to open and endure. Breweries such as Lone Star and the San Antonio Brewing Association (SABA) not only quenched the thirst of the area's immigrant population but would also have an enormous impact on the local economies.

Jeff Holt, who has maintained the website texasbreweries.com for a decade or more, said that he came to several conclusions when compiling information on the early history of breweries in the state: "1. Whenever more than three Germans get together, a keg of beer is involved. 2. If the Germans couldn't find a brewer, they appointed one. 3. Breweries always consolidate." That pretty much sums up the San Antonio area's brewing history starting in the 1840s.

Whether it was the Western Brewery at the Menger Hotel or the San Antonio Brewing Association (later to be known as Pearl Brewing), the area became *the* brewing leader in Texas. No other city came close, even as the twentieth century rolled around; it regained that crown after Prohibition.

However, there were rumblings in Texas in the late nineteenth and early twentieth centuries of curbing and even outright outlawing the consumption of alcohol. Although brewers, distillers and winemakers were able to stave off the idea of Prohibition for decades, it became a reality in 1919. Over the course of the next fourteen years, most breweries in Texas would fold, and in San Antonio it was no different. In fact, the only brewery to really survive was the San Antonio Brewing Association, and it had to completely modify its business operations to do so.

The next six decades were dark ones for those craving something more from their beer than they could get from growing national breweries and an ever-tightening group of companies that owned a fairly large portfolio of homogenous brands through acquisition. This was especially true for the many service men and women who were stationed in or retired to the San Antonio area after previous postings in Germany or England, where full-flavored brewing tradition still abided in some form.

The road to beer redemption, though, was coming. As laws around the country began to change in the United States in the early 1990s, so, too, did they change in the Alamo City. Lone Star and Pearl were still in business as part of larger companies, but the few microbreweries in the state were struggling. In 1993, when laws were passed allowing the legalization of brewpubs, the tide turned. Several brewpubs popped up in San Antonio within a few months, with one of these early brewpubs still in existence today.

Over the next decade or so, small microbreweries and brewpubs would come and go until 2008, when quite a change came to San Antonio: the city's first new brewpub in years opened. What followed in the seven years since is an incredible turn for the better in the area's brewing future. The Greater San Antonio area of Bexar and contiguous counties now boasts about twenty breweries, with several more in the planning stages.

While the days of the great regional brewery are gone for San Antonio, we are now in the midst of a renaissance of sorts, putting the city on the cusp of returning to brewing greatness. Each day sees a growing appreciation and thirst for finely crafted ales and lagers of all styles, as well as the brewers so passionate about their art. It is nothing less than inspiring to look into San Antonio's brewing past even as the present-day snapshot gives us a glimpse into what the future might be.

.

Chapter 1

Brewing on the Banks of the Comal

In March 1847, a letter signed by thirty residents of the fledgling town of New Braunfels was printed in German in the *Galveston Daily News*. It invited Germans and Austrians living in the coastal city to look for their fortunes farther inland in the still-new state of Texas. The "lowlands" of Texas along the Gulf Coast did not have a suitable climate for Europeans, they claimed, and the new community in the Texas Hill Country was on the rise, with extended streets and new houses going up each month in town and on outlying farms.

While the group of immigrants fleeing economic and political hard times in their home country had a rough start from their arrival at the intersection of the pristine Comal and Guadalupe Rivers in 1845, the founders bragged that not only did they have plenty of jobs for mechanics and artisans and fertile farmland, but they also had a mercantile, two doctors, two pharmacists and several bakeries. Also of note for such a young town was the mention of a brewery.

Although the brewery was not mentioned by name, one of the men signing the letter of invitation to would-be settlers was Julius Rennert, a shoemaker from Salzuffeln, Lippe Detmold, Germany (the town is now most commonly spelled "Salzuflen"). Rennert was a cobbler by trade, although a reluctant one by some accounts. He probably made a living making and repairing shoes, and the current owners of the property where he settled found remnants of the tools of his early trade.

Julius Rennert later in life. By this point in his life, he'd been a shoemaker, a brewer and a beer distributor. He was a founder of New Braunfels and one of its leading citizens. *Sophienburg Museum and Archives.*

Brewing was an honored tradition in the Germanic states and beer a part of the everyday diet of business owners and laborers alike, so it should come as no surprise that one of the original settlers of New Braunfels would take up the mash paddle and start making beer for his fellow residents and even settlers in surrounding communities.

During his life in Texas, Rennert served as mayor pro tem of the city and was a member of the men's singing society, where much of his beer was imbibed. The Sophienburg Museum & Archives, in an exhibit presented in early 2015, displayed photos and records that showed locally brewed beer at the center of everyday life in the early years of the settlement, including the singing society practices, the shooting club and gatherings of card players.

"Beer drinking played a fairly significant role in the social and cultural life of early New Braunfels," according to the Sophienburg's curators. "Men frequented saloons to roll dice and catch up on local, state and international news as well as share a few glasses with friends. The newspaper men celebrated the completion of typesetting the daily paper with a bucket of beer. Beer was a part of Schuetzenvereine (shooting clubs) and Gesangvereine (singing clubs), meetings and celebrations. Skat (card) tournaments were accompanied by beer and wine."

When the daily newspaper, *Neu Braunfelser Zeitung*, published a list of local businesses in 1866, it catalogued eleven taverns, a brewery (Rennert's) and a distillery. The Sophienburg found evidence that there also were numerous homebrewers, winemakers and distillers before and after the Civil War among the New Braunfels Germans well into the twentieth century.

It is unclear just when he started brewing and selling his beer to the citizens of New Braunfels, but records show that he paid the German Emigration Company $17.43 for Lot 160 on the banks of the Comal River in 1847. It was in the same block as the lot he drew in the company's lottery when the settlement started in 1845 and where he made his first home. He later purchased part of Lot 159 at a cost of $10.00 to give him access to Comal

The door to the one-time Rennert Brewery is marked with reminders of the many floods that the New Braunfels area has endured over the years. *Michael E. Poling.*

Street so wagons could make their way to stores and taverns of the city for deliveries. In early 1849, Rennert mortgaged all three lots and five acres of farmland he received as one of the first settlers for $3,000.00. Deed records show that it was repaid by March 1852.

In the 1850 Texas census, Rennert's profession was listed as "brewer." The deed records, the loan and the census are the clues that lead the authors to believe that Rennert's may have been the first commercial brewery in Texas, predating San Antonio's Western Brewery—often cited as the first in the state—by at least five years. However, there were nineteen brewers and distillers in the 1850 Texas census but no actual manufacturing licenses on record for breweries or distilleries, according to the Texas State Historical Society's Handbook of Texas Online, which also notes that "this indicates there were people who considered themselves to be in the brewing business, even though they operated only small home breweries."

That leaves the "first brewery" designation a difficult one to determine, but it is probably fair to say that Rennert didn't pay off a $3,000 loan by giving away beer to his friends or by shoemaking and farming. Another New Braunfelser, Johan Schneider, listed in the 1850 census as a brewer, may also have had some trade, but records don't show any later formalization of the brewery in that city; rather, they show a later attempt to get one started in Austin in the late 1850s.

The brewery Rennert eventually built on Lot 160, a larger and more formal affair than where he must have been brewing before, is believed to have been built in about 1855 and produced beer for the region until at least 1879. The brewery still stands much as it did in 1879, as the basement of a residential dwelling. The solidly built rock, brick and cedar-beamed structure was built first to accommodate the brewery, and then the Rennert home was built above it. The Stein family bought the property in 1916 and left the brewery space intact for various uses, including as a lab for developing pool-cleaning chemicals. A modern home now sits on top of the brewery and is still in the Stein family.

A now-closed drive runs behind the house at basement level along the riverbank, where deliveries of hops and grain were made along with wood to stoke the fire for the brew kettle. Barrels of beer left the same way. "Julius spent several years learning the brewery business, conducting his own business interests, as well as farming before he amassed sufficient capital to build his own brewery," recalled the *Neu Braunfels Zeitung* in a September 2, 1886 obituary for the esteemed brewer and city leader. "His grown sons helped him with the brewery operation."

In the drawing "1881 Birdseye View of New Braunfels," a water tower is shown on the brewery property. A water wheel pumped from the spring-fed Comal River to the tower and provided water for brewing and cleaning.

Rennert may have supplied San Antonio saloons with beer, as well as those in the closer, small German communities popping up around New Braunfels. While there is no record of how many barrels he could brew at a time, a newspaper ad from 1878 proclaimed that the brewery "is able to supply large quantities of beer."

While other breweries came and went, usually lasting only two or three years, Rennert prevailed until beer from other cities made its way into the city. Thirsty though it might be, New Braunfels eventually had a glut of competing beer brands, which only intensified when the railroad connected the town to San Antonio, Austin and Houston. Anheuser-Busch and Lone Star advertisements began to show up in the *Zeitung* in the 1880s.

Rennert may have closed the brewery as early as 1879, but other historians believe it could have been in the early 1880s, only a few years before his death. The two eldest sons who helped him in the brewery made their way to the nearby community of Cibolo to farm, and another moved to Cincinnati, Ohio, to work in a brewery. Frank Rennert, the youngest of his ten surviving children, was seventeen when his father died and later became a lawyer in San Antonio, a pioneering cotton broker and a friend of San Antonio brewing magnate Otto Koehler.

When the railhead came to South Texas, some reports say, Julius Rennert used his wagons to become a distributor of the Anheuser-Busch beers coming off the railcars from St. Louis. While the brewery likely provided him with three decades of good income to support a large family, his estate, Comal County probate records show, was worth $45,332 at the time of his death. The assets included farms in several counties and the former brewery and house, but more than $30,000 was from notes he held on loans that he made through a private banking business.

For all his involvement in the history of the region—mayor, justice of the peace, singing society founder, public school founder and a head of the group that helped form one of the state's first public water works—Rennert should be well remembered by history. But it is his role as the artisan providing the lubricant needed to tame the wild land for which he will be most remembered.

Chapter 2

Across the Alley from the Alamo

The Western and Degen Breweries

Around the time Julius Rennert was brewing up *gemütlichkeit*, that German sense of comfort and hospitality particular to a biergarten, for New Braunfels–area residents, William A. Menger of Windecken, Hanau, Germany, was working to do the same thing for the Germans and visitors to San Antonio. Menger's Western Brewery opened in 1855 on Alamo Square (also known as Alamo Plaza), next to the famed Shrine of Texas Liberty, which only nineteen years earlier had been a bloody battleground. Most accounts credit the Western as the first commercially licensed brewery in Texas.

The son of John George Menger, William Menger stood a modest five feet, two inches tall. An experienced cooper and brewer while in Germany, Menger arrived in San Antonio in 1847 after a long transatlantic journey by sea via Galveston, Texas. Upon arriving in the area, Menger didn't find it easy to make a living, working as a handyman among other jobs. Menger started a cooperage soon after arriving in San Antonio, capitalizing on his skills as both a handyman and a brewer.

Menger found lodging as well as his future bride in a nearby boardinghouse on the corner of St. Mary's and Commerce Streets owned by Mary Guenther, a recent widow who also hailed from Germany and had come to Texas with her late husband and her mother, Mrs. Anna Baumanschueter. After only a few months in San Antonio, Mary's husband passed away, leaving her a widow at age twenty-eight. A friendship took root between Menger and the widow Guenther, with romance following soon after. By 1851, the couple had married, and the following year, Menger became a United States citizen.

Livening up the wedding festivities was the realization that their pastor, Reverend Claude Marie Dubuis, had walked from his home in nearby Castroville to San Antonio to perform the ceremony. Upon hearing this, Menger scolded Reverend Dubuis, saying, "Why didn't you tell me you had no horse? I would have gladly sent you a good one!" Dubuis, who a decade later would become the Roman Catholic bishop of Galveston, advised the groom, "If I would have ridden a good horse, the Indians would have killed me to get to the horse, so I preferred to walk."

Menger was quite the civic-minded individual, taking the welfare of his adoptive city seriously. Not only was he a part of the city's volunteer fire department, but he is also credited with bringing the first steam fire engine to the Alamo City. Even as Menger was making his name in San Antonio, the twenty-five-year-old Karl B. "Charles" Degen arrived in Texas from Baden, Mannheim, Germany, in 1850 and made his way to San Antonio. This would be very short-lived, however, as Degen soon relocated to the Medina River area north of Castroville, a German and Alsatian community founded in 1844 by Henry Castro, for work as a farmer. Degen worked hard for two years as a farmer and a cowboy. He is even credited as having brought the first irrigation plant to Texas. Degen tried desperately to make his way in Castroville and his new country. Like so many of his fellow immigrants, he quit and left for California to work in the gold mines that had popped up after the 1849 gold rush.

After trying his hand at mining, Degen left California for South America. Although it is not known how long Degen spent in South America, or even why he was there, he later returned to San Antonio via Panama and may have worked on the Panama Railroad construction.

He is credited as having been the first subscriber to one of San Antonio's earliest papers, the *San Antonio Light*, and likely fought fires alongside Menger as a member of the local volunteer brigade and enjoyed telling tales of his adventures combating flames. In an obituary for the legendary Texas-German brewer in the February 1912 edition of the *Brewer's Journal*, Degen was recalled for his community involvement, which also included membership in the Beethoven Maennerchor, a nonprofit organization founded in 1867 for the purpose of preserving German song, music and language.

Although the society has since moved a few blocks to the south on Alamo Street, it still exists as an active organization in San Antonio's King William District. Not surprisingly, the Beethoven's bar is still a popular spot to drink

German beer and join in beer-drinking songs with the German choirs and band on special occasions such as Oktoberfest, Maifest and San Antonio's citywide, ten-day celebration of Fiesta.

After a few years at its original location, Mary Menger moved the boardinghouse to Alamo Plaza in 1855. Menger longed to open a brewery and founded the Western Brewery that same year next to the boardinghouse, at 204 Alamo Plaza. The ruins of the Alamo, a former Spanish mission turned doomed fortress, were next door to the brewery.

By 1856, Menger needed assistance and recruited Degen as his brewmaster. Little is known at this point about the recipe Degen first used. The young German brewmaster loved his secrets and refused time after time to part with the specific details of the recipe, despite many area bars and hotels clamoring to get it. We can, however, discern a part of it from checking historical records. Business records of the later Menger Hotel revealed that Irish and Californian hops were brought into San Antonio, as well as Blaffer Malt and Guiterman Spalt. Hotel records also reflect that Degen used a "secret ingredient" of piloncillo, a Mexican candy sugar, to give his ale a unique character different from anything found in the strict brewing regimes of his native Germany. (See Appendix B for details on what the recipe may have entailed.)

The success of the brewery was apparent from the very beginning. The Western's beer, which was known to most of the people of the town as "Menger Beer," became so popular in San Antonio and the surrounding areas that some patrons slept on the floor, a bench or even on the bar instead of walking or riding home. The legend maintained by the Menger Hotel is that Degen's beer was so strong that most folks weren't able to walk out of the bar, let alone walk home or even find their horses, prompting the Mengers to build the soon-to-be grand hotel on the site.

If the famed U.S. (and later Confederate) general Robert E. Lee imbibed during his San Antonio encampments in 1856 and 1860, he was most likely drinking beer from the Western Brewery and perhaps from Julius Rennert's brewery thirty miles to the north.

Spurred by that fact and the growing number of visitors to the city, the Mengers decided to forgo their nearby boardinghouse and build a full-fledged hotel. In 1859, the Menger Hotel was opened on the site of the brewery, with the brewery itself moved to the tunnels under the hotel and the entrance at the back of the hotel at 237 Blum Street.

With a world-class menu that featured exotic game meat and a famous turtle soup (with turtles obtained from the local San Antonio River), the

Menger Hotel also served up its famous adult beverage to patrons, who came from all over the Southwest to try it. At that time, there were no other hotels south or west of the Lower Colorado River with the size or opulence of the Menger Hotel. Partly because of the beer and cuisine, it became a popular spot for cattle and cotton traders as the city grew as a regional hub of agricultural commerce.

A key feature of the brewery was its underground tunnels that served as fermentation space, as well as storage for the grain, hops and yeast. With even ales needing a much cooler temperature to ferment than average room temperature in a South Texas summer, these tunnels supplied Degen with just what he needed for his beer. Water for the brewery also was sourced from Alamo Madre Ditch, a water channel dug by Spanish monks in the 1700s that ran through the Menger property. The main tunnels were continuously used until the 1940s, when they were filled in with dirt during a renovation of the hotel.

Several history buffs and even professional historians have tried to get a look into parts of the tunnels that are still open but have been denied by hotel officials. Some claim safety and liability reasons, while some hotel staff believe that they may be the most haunted part of a hotel that already lays claim to ghosts seen on guest floors and credited with disturbing glassware in the hotel bar and restaurant. One prominent San Antonio historian told the authors that a staff member "turned white" and was visibly disturbed by the suggestion that anyone would want to visit the tunnels.

During its heyday, the Western served not only as a meeting place for community patrons but also as a place for San Antonio's money elite and politicians to discuss politics and important topics of the day.

In 1871, just sixteen years after the brewery's opening, William Menger died from an illness. Mary Menger continued to run the hotel after his death, while Degen maintained the brewing side of the operation on Blum Street until 1878, at which point brewing ceased at the Menger. The year it closed, the Western Brewery was the largest brewery in Texas, producing 1,666 barrels that year, with the next largest in Brenham between San Antonio and Houston.

Degen moved the brewery to 344 East Crockett Street and Blum, which was behind his home, in about 1879. The site is now occupied by the later extension of the Menger Hotel and adjacent Rivercenter Mall. Degen may not have taken the old brewing equipment with him when he started his own brewery. Sitting on a ranch in the Southeast Bexar County town

As visitors to the Menger Hotel walk over the black-and-white-tiled foyer entering the hotel, few realize that they are walking over the original location of the Western Brewery before the hotel was built in 1859. *Jeremy Banas.*

of Elmendorf are the weather-beaten remnants of the Western Brewery, handed down through various family members.

Although what happened with the original equipment isn't documented, Roy Wahne, the grandson of Catherine Edith Menger, came into possession of these pieces of brewing history. Catherine Menger was the daughter of William A. Menger's son Peter Gustav Menger, who was born the same year the hotel opened and just four years after the opening of the brewery.

Wahne said that he remembers first coming across the equipment on the property of his Uncle Gus, who had received the equipment from his mother, Catherine. "I remember first finding the equipment stashed in my uncle's barn years ago," Wahne said. "My uncle offered it to me but let my cousin hold on to it" until he eventually moved it to the Wahne ranch. He fondly remembered stories of the family's involvement in the hotel throughout the years. "My grandmother would talk about how proud she was of our family's history and involvement in the hotel," Wahne said. "Ironically enough, though, some of the brewing equipment was used around the ranch over time as a water trough for the horses." Wahne said that he plans to restore the equipment in the near future for display at his home.

Charles Degen stands at center in this photo with unknown members of his brewing staff. Taken in 1902 at his brewery on Blum Street, it was the same year the United States Health Bulletin declared his beer the purest and best beer to drink in the country. *UTSA Libraries Special Collections.*

A bit worse for the wear, some of Charles Degen's original brewing equipment at the Western Brewery sits on the ranch of the great-great-grandson of William A. Menger. Plans are to restore and display it. *Jeremy Banas.*

Degen's own brewery, when it opened in 1879, was considered one of the biggest purveyors of beer in San Antonio at the time, but this did not last long. The first trains had already arrived in 1877, bringing in competing ales and lagers from around the country, including the already-famous Budweiser from St. Louis, Missouri–based Anheuser-Busch. With many of these lagers weighing in as less expensive and lower in alcohol, Degen's beer was soon overshadowed.

Despite this, Degen continued to thrive, reportedly content with his middle-class existence in San Antonio society, and kept his new brewery a small and simple operation. Degen's beer even received perhaps its highest praise from a very unlikely source: the United States government. In 1902, the *United States Health Bulletin* proclaimed Degen beer to be the best in the country. "The result of laboratory investigation has proven the proper beer to drink and the purest and best to be the beer from the Charles Degen Brewery of San Antonio, Texas." In fact, it was even hailed as a curative beverage for both women and children. This endorsement would only serve to add to Degen's already well-established and almost legendary reputation.

Degen brewed only for his tavern, despite continued requests from many saloons around San Antonio. His outlook on the whole idea amounted to

Visitors to San Antonio's River Center Mall and Menger Hotel often walk by the now bricked-up entrance to Menger and Degen's Western Brewery, part of the hidden history not on the regular downtown tour. *Jeremy Banas.*

being happy just getting to make the beer that he and so many had come to love. Large profits and extravagant lifestyle were not what he desired, instead preferring to make just enough to keep his operation going and enjoy a modest living. He kept a tight ship at his little tavern, not tolerating anyone who became intoxicated.

Degen continued to brew until his death at the age of eighty-seven on February 8, 1912, at which time his son Louis took over as brewmaster until the start of Prohibition. Charles Degen was so passionate about the impending likelihood of the prohibition of alcohol that he has been famously quoted as saying that "if Prohibition comes, Germans in this state will have to form a trust and drink up all the water." When Prohibition hit, Louis Degen made the decision to close the brewery for good, thus ending the last link to San Antonio's brewing origins.

Chapter 3

The Independents

W hat was started by Rennert, Menger and Degen caught on like wildfire in San Antonio. The thirsts of San Antonians were finally being quenched by their own locally made brews, but they required more. Texans have always been proud of anything made in Texas, and beer was no different, especially with the demand from the growing German population. That led to a spate of new breweries over the following fifty years.

While two grew into major operations, most lasted only two or three years, with only a few consolidating into larger operations. Some weren't big enough to do significant marketing and advertising, as Pearl and Lone Star would do, so they also left very little behind about their history. There are some whose names have been lost, known only by the name of the brewer. By the mid-1870s, there were a dozen or more breweries in business in the Greater San Antonio area, including Boerne and New Braunfels.

For three decades, Menger and Degen were nearly the only game in town until the mid-1870s, when several other breweries popped up, including the William Esser Brewery in 1874. Esser's brewery lasted a decade until he sold to St. Louis beer magnate Adolphus Busch for what would develop into the Alamo City Brewing Association and Lone Star.

When land behind the Old Lone Star Brewery, now the San Antonio Museum of Art complex, was being excavated for the Museum Reach of the San Antonio River Walk, archaeologists from the University of Texas–San Antonio found a cache of beer bottles, probably dumped behind a retaining wall in the late 1800s and eventually paved over with a parking lot. The bottles bore the name of William Esser.

The Joseph Hutzler Brewery opened in 1874 and was in business until 1878. Hutzler, who hailed from the French/German-disputed region of Alsace, was a tinsmith. In the 1860s, he traveled to Mexico and, years later, took up brewing after returning to San Antonio.

The Lareoda & Beau Brewery was open initially only from 1878 until 1879, but it later reopened in 1884 and remained open until Prohibition.

The next decade saw several more breweries open, including Alamo Ice and Brewing Company and Alamo Brewery. Alamo Ice and Alamo Brewery would be later consolidated with the Alamo Brewing Association and Anheuser-Busch's Lone Star Brewery.

Breweries like Degen's had no real competition until the late 1870s, when the first train rolled into San Antonio bringing brews from around the country, including the already well-known Budweiser from St. Louis–based Anheuser-Busch. Despite the out-of-town competition, Charles Degen continued to thrive at his little brewery on Blum Street. City Brewery opened in 1881, even after the railroad seemed a major threat to the local industry.

The 1890s saw only a few additions to the brewing family in San Antonio, including the Ochs and Aschbacher Weiss Beer and Porter Brewery from 1890 to 1904 and Frio Brewing, which opened in 1894. However, the date of Frio's close is not known. It likely closed well before Prohibition began. What we do know is that the brewery, whose name would later be used by another independent brewery a century later, was associated with the Alamo

Alamo Brewery

MAKES THE BEST

Pale Vienna and Bavarian

Bottled or Lager Beer.

SURPASSES EVERY BEER IN THE MARKET

════ASK FOR IT════

SPECIAL ATTENTION GIVEN TO FAMILY TRADE.

Very indicative of the times, this late 1800s advertisement for Alamo Brewery (later absorbed into Lone Star) touted its lager as the best. *From* Street, Avenue and Alley Guide to San Antonio, Texas, *edited by Jules A. Appler, 1892. City of San Antonio.*

Brewing Association, meaning Frio was possibly absorbed by the brewing giant and shut down as a brand.

To the southwest of San Antonio, in Castroville, Louis Huth was brewing beer at some point after he settled in the community sometimes called "Little Alsace." The little brewery inside Huth's general store closed in 1863, when he moved to San Antonio. In 1875, Blaise Keiffer opened a brewery in Castroville slightly larger than Huth's operation, but it only lasted nine years. After the brewer's death in 1880, his wife, Louise, ran the brewery for four years.

In the town of Boerne, records show that from 1874 to 1877 Martin Stricht operated a brewery, which Hammer & Buelle took over and ran until 1882. Also in Kendall County, the city of Comfort had its own beer for a few years in the form of the Ingenhuett Brewery, which was open from 1878 to about 1884. German immigrants Thomas and Martin Ingenhuett set up the facility on the banks of Cypress Creek. Their brother, Pete, ran a hotel in the town.

New Braunfels brewing likewise saw a cavalcade of brewing establishments going up against Rennert. At about the same time as Rennert started brewing, Johan Schneider was listed as a brewer and could have been selling in New Braunfels. But by 1858, he had decided to try building a solid brewery in Austin. Schneider was killed in a carriage accident in 1862 in Austin and never saw more than his vaulted beer cellars completed.

Also in the early 1850s, Richard and August Weinert were reported to brew for New Braunfels residents, but records say that they primarily ran a bakery and mercantile, where they also sold sweet wines, cider and gin, some of which could have been made in-house. By the 1860 census, they were known primarily as merchants, and beer would have been very much a side project.

Others who left little trace were Charles Dampmann and Mathias Esser, both brewing in 1860s New Braunfels.

Karl H. Guenther's brewery, which likely lasted for a few years in the 1860s, had a little more notoriety because of his role in the community. In 1853, he married the widow of fellow town founder Jean Jacques von Coll. That marriage came with much land, a house and a store. The businessman, who was listed as "landlord" in the 1860 census, was one of two teachers when the city started a public school in 1854 and was early director of the Germania Saengerverein singing society. He also was a prominent figure in *Der Frei Verein*, or the Free Society, of German Texans. He served as president of that organization in 1854, when it adopted a platform objecting to slavery, but he later served as a captain in Texas forces that fought for the Confederacy.

At some point after the Civil War, Guenther "pursued his father's trade, master brewer, and planned a brewery on the bank of the Comal at the foot of Bridge Street. The work was interrupted by his death in 1870," as reported by the *New Braunfels Herald* newspaper in a Civil War centennial edition in 1961.

The ruins of that brewery were still standing in 1961 but today have been washed away by the force of several floods in the five decades since. Stephen Guenther, the great-great-grandson of the one-time brewer, said that stories handed down by the family have the widow Margarethe Guenther running the brewery after her husband's death. "From all accounts, she was an astute businesswoman," and even served as brewmaster, Stephen Guenther says.

One of the more colorful places in pre-Prohibition New Braunfels was the Phoenix Saloon, built by John Sippel in 1871. He lived on the second floor of the building, while Christian Hohmann and Henry Meier operated a bar and billiards hall on the ground level. From 1872 until 1875, H.R. Schumacker (which sometimes appears spelled "Schuhmacker") operated a brewery in the basement of the building at Castell and Seguin Streets. Schumacker's beer sold for $2.25 per keg, with a glass going for $0.05. A relative may have opened a brewery elsewhere in town for a few years in the early 1880s.

Numerous people ran the saloon portion of the building over the years, but it mostly stayed as some form of the Phoenix Saloon for many years. It has since returned to its roots with a bar that pays homage to the area brewing scene featuring regional beers and music after years as a department store and office services shop. In the late 1880s, between the saloon and the Ludwig Hotel was a beer garden with a small pond, goldfish, catfish and a baby alligator. It was there that the ladies of the town, who couldn't enter the saloons, would gather to enjoy a local beer or wine.

By 1900, the breweries of New Braunfels were gone, but there were numerous saloons, including seventeen in a two-block stretch of downtown.

The city of Seguin, the county seat of neighboring Guadalupe County, has no record of a brewery until 1884, when C.A. Schmidt set up shop. Schmidt brewed until 1877, the same year F.F. Weber picked up the mash paddle and brewed under his name until 1884. From 1878 to 1879, C.P. Krause made beer.

There were eight saloons in Seguin by 1884, but after the closure of the Krause brewery, most were likely serving beer from San Antonio or from the big breweries to the east. It wasn't until 1902 that Seguin had its own brewery again in the form of Pilsner Brewing Company, which lasted until 1907.

After the turn of the century, San Antonio continued to see breweries fall by the wayside even as others opened. Few lasted long in the face of competition. Bongo & Weisse Beer Bottling Works and Manufacturing Company and Brewery at 309 Third Street lasted from 1902 to 1903. Brown Beer Brewing Company made it from 1903 to 1905. Pfieffer & Huhn Brewing was another short-timer, lasting only from 1905 to 1906. Bergman & Walz Brewery and the Albert Drankowi Brewery each lasted from 1906 to 1907, while Beck's Muenchener Weiss Beer Company Brewery picked up the mash paddle in 1907 and closed the following year.

Geo. Aschbacher Brewery continued the business of the former Ochs and Aschbacher Weiss Beer and Porter Brewery after 1904, when Lorenz Ochs was no longer part of the operation. Aschbacher lasted longer than many from that time, brewing until 1914. Schober Ice and Brewing Company, which opened in 1905, also had a good run, closing its doors with Prohibition.

Print and photographic evidence still exists for the Peter Brothers Brewery, and by all accounts, it appears to have been quite popular in the midst of a frenzy of openings and closings. Despite that, the brewery was in business just five years from 1905 to 1910. One former patron remembered it nostalgically: "Carlos Payne stood in front of Schilo's [restaurant] on E. Commerce, looked east toward Joske's [department store] and recalled the days when he used to amble over to the old Peters Brewery on Commerce and Water and pay the mustachioed bartender 15 cents for a ham and cheese on rye and a big mug of beer," the *San Antonio Light* reported in an undated article.

In New Braunfels, as the possibility of alcohol prohibition became more likely, the New Braunfels Brewing Company opened its doors to provide the first local beers in two decades to slake the thirsts of the town founders' descendants and newcomers.

When Prohibition did arrive, the "modern" brewery continued brewing, putting out its version of non-alcoholic brew. Signs around the town noted, "There is no beer near here, but there is near beer here." Its near beer, dubbed Busto, may have been mostly devoid of alcohol, but there were apparently special deliveries made to certain customers until federal law enforcement caught on and closed the brewery down in 1925 for selling beer with alcohol. The building still exists as the meat processing and smoking

Members of the Peter Brothers brewing family are seen here taking a break in their brewhouse to pose for a photo. The brothers had become quite popular due to their brew but fell victim to stiff competition and closed a mere five years after opening. *UTSA Libraries Special Collections.*

facility for New Braunfels Smokehouse, which has an international mail-order business.

Perhaps the most successful and popular of these small independent breweries was City Brewery, which opened in the early 1880s. Founded and owned by well-known San Antonio resident J.B. Belohradsky, City Brewery began with a vision to be the next great brewery in the United States. The three-story building was outfitted with the latest brewing equipment and technologies and was considered a modern marvel of the times. The brewery was built on eight acres near River Avenue, later known as Broadway. It is possible that Belohradsky founded City Brewery in 1881, but construction on the brewery began in 1883.

Chicago architect H.H. Alford designed and oversaw construction of the new brewery, which began in September 1883, when the cornerstone of the building was laid. An unknown publication of the time referenced the

The City Brewery, founded in 1883, not only would house San Antonio's second modernized brewery but also would, in a few short years, become the first home of the San Antonio Brewing Association. *UTSA Libraries Special Collections.*

year-long construction effort of Belohradsky, who "from the start fixed his determination to make a pure unadulterated lager beer, manufactured by Bohemian methods…the water used in the manufacture of this beer from the springs at the head-water where it was absolutely pure and unmixed with any deleterious substance."

Although he didn't advertise often, probably because money was tight after the major investment in the brewery and equipment, word soon spread about this new lager beer from City Brewery, the first well-known lager to be brewed in San Antonio. Despite its authenticity to old-world brewing methods and its popularity, City Brewery's end was not far away. The reason for its demise had nothing to do with beer production but rather a scandal that erupted in 1885, when Belohradsky stood accused of financial improprieties.

Chapter 4

Pearl Brewery

1886-1918 and Prohibition

$\mathbf{B}$ reweries in San Antonio came and went in the way that many businesses do, rarely outliving their founders or the economic forces around them. The exception to the rule was the brewery that would come to be known as Pearl. It was considered a jewel in San Antonio's industrial crown in the late 1800s and well into the next century until Prohibition, later rising to prominence again by the 1950s. Over the course of nearly 115 years in business as a San Antonio brewery, Pearl had five distinct periods.

The first period began with J.B. Belohradsky's City Brewery on the banks of the San Antonio River. City had been gaining steam since its 1883 opening. Decked out in the latest in brewing technology, the brewery didn't have to spend much money on advertising because the local newspapers seemed happy to talk up the new brewery. What's more, he was selling his beer for $3.50 per keg, as much as a dollar less than competing beers coming in by rail and gaining popularity. But City Brewery and its owner soon came under assault from sources outside the city, a seemingly insurmountable amount of debt and a scarcity of capital.

A Polish benevolent society in Chicago that had once employed Belohradsky came knocking with allegations of financial improprieties. The allegations of embezzlement may have been politically motivated; nevertheless, it began to consume the beer maker. Relying heavily on his lawyer, a young and ambitious man, Belohradsky was able to successfully fight allegations meant to cripple him. It was enough, however, to make his shareholders nervous. By 1886, it seemed that the popular City Brewery was in trouble. Despite successfully defending his name, Belohradsky's scandal and mounting debt meant turning over City Brewery to a receiver in the late fall of 1886.

Waiting in the wings was none other than his own attorney, Oscar Bergstrom. Under the guise of assistance, Bergstrom, Belohradsky and a small group of businessmen met to see if an influx of cash could save the brewery. One of the men at the meeting was a young Otto Koehler, even though he was employed at the competing Lone Star Brewing as a manager. While the bailout was unsuccessful, Bergstrom-enlisted Koehler and local businessmen John Jay Stevens and Otto Wahrmund formed an ownership group to buy City Brewery out from under Belohradsky for $51,910.96. The deal was closed in February 1887. Later that same year, Belohradsky cleared his debts and left San Antonio.

Now firmly in control of City Brewery, Bergstrom and his partners continued to operate under the name of City Brewery until August 1887, when they were recharged under the moniker of San Antonio Brewing Association, a name that can still be seen carved in stone over the door of the main brewery building. As a lawyer, Bergstrom was known for his oratory, and his appearance was that of a dapper man in a silk plug hat, with a gardenia flower in his lapel. His wealth stemmed from earlier investment in railroads and mining, two industries that were building the West. It is believed that the twenty-seven-year-old Bergstrom is the one who lured Otto Koehler away from the brewery's rival.

As control changed at City Brewery, Otto Koehler withdrew his investment in Lone Star and threw his cash into the new ownership group. He also was successful in purchasing a beer recipe from the Kaiser-Beck Brewery in Bremen, Germany. It would be the first known international sale of a trade name and gave SABA the right to use the Pearl name in association with the beer. Drawing from his time at Lone Star and listening to the callings of the local German population, Koehler and the San Antonio Brewing Association wanted to offer what they felt might be a lighter, more refreshing beer than the still dominant ales of the time. The commercial refrigeration at the brewery not only allowed for the making of the crisp lagers Germans were used to, but they also could be brewed year-round without worrying about the blistering South Texas summers.

Koehler certainly wasn't new to the brewing field when he arrived in San Antonio in 1884 from St. Louis, Missouri. Koehler had first worked at Griesedieck Brewery (a precursor to Falstaff Brewing) as a bookkeeper. Koehler had a head for business and likely met Anton Griesedieck through his brother August Koehler's connections. Koehler spent two years at Griesedieck, where he took a shine to the brewing industry in addition to meeting and marrying Emma Bentzen.

Around this time, Adolphous Busch, who had already built a reputation in St. Louis and the Midwest with his ownership in Anheuser-Busch Brewing, sought to lay claim to the rest of the country's taste buds and beer money. Very much like the future incarnations of Anheuser-Busch, Adolphus Busch was developing partnerships around the country to open or buy regional breweries that would brew different beers than his famed Budweiser. Busch, along with other investors, started the Lone Star Brewing Association in San Antonio. Busch hired Koehler in 1884 to go to San Antonio and help run Lone Star.

Soon after taking control of City, the association released Pearl beer, which was often referred to as City XXX Pearl Beer. Named for the so-called pearl-like bubbles resulting from the carbonation, the beer made its debut on July 4, 1887. It turned out to be genius marketing The XXX on the label, since medieval times, had been used to designate the quality of the beer produced by European monasteries, with XXX being the highest quality. A brewery representative in 1887 hyped the new beer in print, invoking both the old names for the beer people had become used to and the new name. "The new City Beer, just out, and very fine, try it. Have you tried the new brand of City Pearl Beer? The finest flavored beer in the market. Be sure and try, and you will be convinced. Warranted to be the same at all times. Ask for it, drink no other."

O. BERGSTROM, Pres.   O. WAHRMUND, Supt.   O. KOEHLER, V. P. and Mgr.

X X X PEARL BEER

EXCELLED BY NONE
EQUAL TO THE VERY BEST
Try it

SABA ad from the late 1800s advertising Pearl XXX beer. *From* Street, Avenue and Alley Guide to San Antonio, Texas, *edited by Jules A. Appler, 1892. City of San Antonio.*

The brewery quickly gained in popularity, delivering its new Pearl beer all over San Antonio, much to the delight of the city's thirsty residents. Production soon increased exponentially, necessitating some upgrades and expansion. Part of these upgrades included the installation of more modern refrigeration equipment brought in from Chicago. By late 1888, the brewery included other infrastructure such as offices, a cooper shop, a washing house, a bottling building and storage rooms, in addition to the already existing hop room and beer cellars. Several years later, a wagon shed was added, and the cooper shop and bottling building were expanded.

It was one thing to buy a recipe that would wow German Texans. It was quite another to make it work every time. That was made possible with the help of a new brewmaster, Oscar Oswald Schreiber of Chicago, best known for his role as brewmaster at Schlitz Brewing. Brewing a consistent and lighter-bodied beer turned out to be a hit and would be the beginning of Pearl's regional dominance.

Although he had already become involved behind the scenes at City Brewing, Koehler officially resigned from Lone Star in 1887. He and Emma Koehler took up residence in the Ward 5 of San Antonio, a location near downtown and the brewery. The brewery wasn't in the best of shape, and considerable money had to be spent on improvements. But buying an existing brewery rather than starting their own gave them an entity already well known in the city, as well as previously established distribution networks and connections with vendors.

Despite a prominent role in San Antonio Brewing Association's beginnings and his almost honorary title of president, Bergstrom left San Antonio and headed for New York City, choosing instead to focus on his other investments and leaving the burgeoning brewery to Koehler's oversight. It was an opportunity Koehler wasted no time capitalizing on. Koehler quickly set a tone for the company, one that would carry it far into the next century. Koehler and his partners continued Belohradsky's mantra, using local resources for the brewery's ingredients and purchasing goods and service from the local citizenry. Koehler would later institute many employee-friendly policies that would endear employees to the association well into the future. It seems that it wasn't just the beer that Koehler and the gang sought to improve but how the brewery was run as well.

With the new ownership firmly in place, the affairs of the brewery were left in the hands of Koehler and Wahrmund. Bergstrom, though president of the association, was already focusing more on his other ventures and less on the brewery. City continued to brew and sell the remaining pilsner that was left from Belohradsky's time. Koehler even used Belohradsky's existing distribution routes and sent City beer to the far reaches of Texas, as well as New Mexico.

In April 1887, the first period of Pearl's history came to an end. At this time, the brewery was officially approved for a new charter and was officially renamed the San Antonio Brewing Association. For decades, the association used April 1887 as its origin date. It wasn't until after Prohibition ended that the year 1886 was more commonly used as the date of the brewery's genesis, perhaps to indicate when the association formed and not when the title actually passed into the member's hands.

A rare drawing of San Antonio Brewing Association president Otto Koehler, made in his later years. *UTSA Libraries Special Collections.*

Brewmaster Oswald Schreiber quickly bonded with his new employer. Utilizing a solid lager recipe, years of experience and his proximity to San Antonio's fresh water, Schreiber was confident that he could maintain the quality he had at Schlitz and then some. Once its new flagship beer began its run, it's reported that Pearl XXX grew famous quickly enough that it was on tap at the 1893 World's Fair in Chicago to quench the thirst of attendees.

With the new equipment upgrades—such as a new cellar, additional ice machine and a boiler in the brewery—San Antonio Brewing Association was at least as modern a brewery as nearby neighbor Lone Star. And the brewery was putting out about one hundred barrels of beer per day. These upgrades did not come cheap, and the brewery looked to its shareholders for $80,000 to make the improvement. No doubt they appreciated the ability to cool the wort and finished product this efficiently, instead of relying on underground tunnels, as Menger and Degen were doing even a decade earlier.

As San Antonio Brewing Association's popularity rose, more and more support arose for the little brewery in San Antonio. One show of support came from the infamous Judge Roy Bean, who served only Pearl in his bar, where he meted out justice as "Law West of the Pecos." Bean's obsession with actress and singer Lilly Langtry was well known and served many years later as inspiration for naming the bar and event venue in the converted horse stables the Jersey Lilly, the name under which Langtry performed.

Production and distribution had increased exponentially by 1889, and the board of the San Antonio Brewing Association determined that its horse-drawn wagons were not efficient enough to reach its wide geographic distribution. What it needed was a rail system. Not having easy access to San Antonio's fledgling rail system, Koehler and the board built their own. Although the electric car system was small, it allowed beer to be transported to the nearby lines of the Southern Pacific Railroad. It also delivered raw materials for beer making from inbound trains.

By 1892, production at the brewery had reached about sixty thousand barrels a year and took more than sixty employees to run. The following year, Pearl's demand for production had outgrown the existing brewhouse. The *San Antonio Daily Light* reported in 1893 that "the City Brewing Company has now in contemplation extensive enlargements as they feel justified by their success and increasing demand for their product in doubling their capacity. The plans for a new brewing house of latest design, additional storage vault for 10,000 bottles, new stables for horses, are now in the hands of the architects, the buildings to be built of brick and iron and fireproof." The architect referred to by the *Daily Light* was famed brewery architect August Maritzen of Chicago. It's not known exactly how the San Antonio Brewing Association was made aware of Maritzen other than reputation, but some speculate that Koehler may have met him through his work prior to the association. The brewhouse was completed in late 1894, with the stables completed the same year. The stables have become as iconic as the brewhouse itself. Designed as an elliptical shape, it had windows all around and today serves as a high-end event center.

The four-year, $250,000 expansion added a new bottling house, a wash house, an ice plant, a new beer vault, a boiler room, a stockroom and a modernization of the cellars. The new brewhouse held twenty-nine wooden tanks, each holding 250 barrels, and eight 600-barrel horizontal wooden tanks. There was also room for about ten thousand bottles.

San Antonio Brewing Association seemed to be on a roll, despite rival Lone Star also expanding and the venerable Charles Degen still putting out the beer that had helped build early San Antonio. But it also was a time when the rumblings of going dry began in earnest, something dreaded by all those who enjoyed or made beer. In 1893, the Anti-Saloon League, born in Ohio, would blossom like no other temperance group seen before, with more subtle and effective tactics. With its close to 5 million members, the Anti-

Saloon League worked through the political machine to flex its muscles and sometimes frighten folks into agreeing with the anti-alcohol movement. This thought process would resound with many traditional Christians in Texas and would lead to the state's own prohibition of alcohol starting before the federal government passed it into law.

The time to worry was not yet at hand, and the San Antonio Brewing Association was knee deep in the expansion of its brewery. Even with a somewhat reduced capacity during construction, the San Antonio Brewing Association produced nearly forty-nine thousand barrels of beer, approximately 40 percent of total beer production in Texas for the year.

By the time the expanded brewery opened in 1884, San Antonio was considered the richest city in the state, and brewery output neared 100,000 barrels for the year. An article published on December 22, 1894, in the *San Antonio Daily Light* announced the completion of the Maritzen-designed brewhouse by the San Antonio Foundry Company. The stables, designed by local architect Otto Kramer, were also completed that year. Kramer, another transplant from the Midwest, was already well known for designing the San Antonio City Hall, completed in 1892. Expansion continued into 1895 with construction of the engine room and boiler house. That took another $150,000, borrowed from the St. Louis Trust Company and a mortgage on the land. The engine room, which borders the brewhouse, also was designed by Maritzen.

The expansion didn't stop there. The next addition to the rapidly growing brewery complex was a Maritzen-designed stock house, with local architect Albert Beckmann hired to manage all construction efforts. An excerpt from an unidentified local paper in 1897 gives a bit of insight into the operation: "The plans for the magnificent new stockhouse for the City Brewery are in the hands of Architect Beckmann who is getting them ready for bids soon. The structure will be 61 x 75 feet, 5 and 6 stories high or 9 x 170 feet respectively: tower 125 feet to flagstaff. It will be an all steel 'Chicago' construction, enclosed with brick and the installation of walls will be superior to anything in the country, pitch filling in exterior walls and hollow tiles being employed." With the original City brewhouse occupying space right near the stock house, the "old" building was demolished to make room.

The San Antonio Brewing Association was dealt a tragic blow in 1899: brewmaster Oscar Oswald Schreiber died at the age of fifty. The man who valued quality more than he did quantity would be succeeded by his apprentice, Gottfried Schobel, who would brew at San Antonio Brewing Association until he left in 1904.

Up until 1904, the San Antonio Brewing Association's offices comprised several nearby buildings. As the brewery itself grew, so did the need for a consolidated administrative space. This need was satisfied with the completion of a new office building in 1904 off the brewery entrance on James Street. Otto Koehler took over the presidency of the organization in 1899 after Bergstrom moved to New York City. Koehler, Wahrmund, J.J. Stevens and their attorney bought out the other partners in the association during a 1901 rechartering, and that set the stage for Koehler's notoriety, wealth and mastery of a brewery operation to stand as a shining example of modern American industrialization.

As the breweries in the state grew larger and competition stiffened, San Antonio Brewing Association joined with Lone Star Brewing Company, Texas Brewing Company of Fort Worth, American Brewing Association of Houston and the Houston Ice and Brewing Company to form the Texas Consolidated Brewing Association. Through a joint stock ownership program, the breweries hoped to stabilize beer prices. Each member agreed not to partake in discount pricing and to price its beer at no less than $2.50 per barrel. This was considered quite an accomplishment by some, as price fixing at that level hadn't yet occurred in railroads, oil and other industries. The price fixing by the beer barons of Texas, however, eventually led to a state antitrust case that would cost the breweries dearly in the years before they had to shut down brewing operations altogether.

Initially operating its advertising much like Belohradsky had, San Antonio Brewing Association rarely advertised its beer, with the exception of Pearl. In 1903, however, two of its other brands, Muenchener and Texas Pride, were added to the advertising plan. By 1905, Texas Pride had become a preference among some, although what the beer's flavor or style were is not known. Labels from 1905 read, "Our new extra fine Texas Pride."

By 1903, the threat of the dry camp was growing stronger. San Antonio Brewing Association and the rest of the members of the Texas Consolidated Brewing Association, along with Dallas Brewing Company and Galveston Brewing Company, joined as the Texas Brewers' Association to fund a campaign combating the growing sentiment of banning all alcohol. To this end, money was donated to the campaigns of those who were friendly to the "wet" camp. Each company pledged twenty cents per barrel sold to gain favor with judges who might be called on to rule on contested elections, state and federal legislative candidates and the governor. That money helped usher Oscar Branch into the Governor's Mansion in Austin, which led to the nickname of "Budweiser Branch" given to him by his dry camp opponents. San Antonio Brewing Association co-founder Otto Warhmund also won a seat in the Texas legislature and was elected three more times after that for eight years in the House of Representatives.

Not able to focus solely on the growing "dry" sentiment in Texas, the brewery forged ahead in planning for the future. Otto and Emma Koehler took a trip to Germany to bring back their nephew and future association president Otto A. Koehler, the son of the elder Otto's twin brother, Ralph.

The next few years would see innovations and changes in the brewery, as well as strikes among the workers. By 1910, San Antonio Brewing Association had moved from wooden to steel barrels, added an enzyme at the end of the brewing process that clarified the beer's natural haziness and survived a workers' strike. Fortunately, the strike lasted only one day, May 6, 1910, with an agreement having been reached to increase pay by two dollars per week and institute a standardized work schedule.

By 1911, the debate over "wet" versus "dry" was decades old, and those in favor of dry laws were gaining steam. In Texas, dry legislation was mostly supported by rural counties, but it also had many legislators on its side. Leading the charge for supporters of the current wet way of life was Governor Branch, who went so far as to cut funding for the enforcement of dry laws in the counties where they already existed. Not giving up, dry supporters in the legislature had the matter put up for a vote; it passed in the House but soon stalled in the Senate. Wet legislators broke the Senate quorum by having eleven senators hide out in San Antonio at the ranch of San Antonio Brewing Association attorney Fred C. Goeth. The bill officially failed in July 1911.

By 1913, the Anti-Saloon League had gone national, marching on Washington, D.C., with a petition asking for a constitutional amendment in favor of alcohol prohibition. By 1915, the petition had become a bill and was voted on (197 in favor and 190 against). The league had enough votes to prove a point, even if it was not enough to become law.

Otto Koehler would not live to see the outcome of the battle over beer and booze and how it would affect his beloved San Antonio Brewing Association. On Sunday night, November 12, 1914, Koehler was shot by one of his mistresses in the cottage he had purchased for her, joining his mentor, Adolphous Busch, who had passed away earlier that year. Emma Burgemeister would later be indicted by a grand jury for his death.

The tales of Koehler's death would today read like tabloid journalism or have the makings of a *Dateline* murder mystery thanks to conflicting versions of just how Koehler was killed. Almost immediately after Koehler's death, the story of "the three Emmas" surfaced, with the papers revealing that he had three women named Emma in his life: his wife and two mistresses. The affairs appear to have begun in 1910 after Emma Koehler was involved in an auto accident that left her injured and in need of care. Otto hired nurse Emma Dumpke, who was described in one account as a "pretty, petite brunette," to take care of his wife. Soon after, an affair appears to have begun between Dumpke and Koehler, even as the two women became close. At some point, a fellow nurse and friend of Dumpke's came to visit her at the Koehler house. Dumpke told her friend, Emma Hedda Burgemeister, of her affair with Koehler. Soon Burgemeister joined the love triangle, and Koehler bought a cottage for them on Hunstock Street, off South Presa Street. He paid Dumpke's expenses and gave her $125 per week in spending money. Burgemeister received $50 a week when she joined Dumpke in the house.

That arrangement was kept for several years, until Dumpke advised Koehler that she was getting married. For some unknown reason, possibly to avoid being alone, Koehler proposed to Burgemeister. She turned him down, citing his wife's condition and not wanting to leave a helpless and injured woman by herself with no means. On that fateful Sunday afternoon

The home of Otto and Emma Koehler sits today much as it did in the late 1800s and early 1900s. During Prohibition, many parties were held at the mansion, which had a "secret" speakeasy. *Jeremy Banas.*

in November, Koehler drove to the cottage by horse and buggy to see Burgemeister. He pushed past Dumpke and went straight to the bedroom, where Burgemeister was lying in bed with a cold rag on her forehead. Soon after, Koehler was dead on the floor with bullets in his heart, face and neck. Burgemeister would later testify that she and Koehler had gotten into an argument and that she shot him to defend herself and Dumpke. At the scene, where there were two pistols and a case knife on the floor near the body, Burgemeister was bleeding from a self-inflicted cut on her wrist. During the trial, she testified that after she shot him, she put the gun to her own head and pulled the trigger. The prosecutor quipped that her "aim at Mr. Koehler was better than your aim at yourself."

The family's version of the story to the press was that there was a dispute over a bill Burgemeister had submitted for care of Emma Koehler. That cover story was soon forgotten as more facts emerged about Koehler's relationship with the women. A grand jury chose not to indict Dumpke but did push through the charges of murder against Burgemeister. Instead, she headed for Europe to use her nursing skills, helping wounded soldiers as World War I raged across that continent. For whatever reason, she returned to San Antonio after the war and stood trial in 1918. After a grand spectacle of a trial, she was found not guilty by an all-male jury. After the trial, she moved to New Orleans and married one of the jurors. One report notes that she even moved back with her new husband to the house where the death occurred because the house had been deeded to her by Koehler years before.

As one of its most prominent citizens, the death of Otto Koehler stunned the entire city. His funeral was held at his three-story mansion on West Ashby Place, followed by a huge funeral procession throughout the streets of downtown. A few days later, a special meeting of the brewery's board of directors was held, mourning Koehler as both a friend and a leader. The board decided at that time to leave the presidency vacant but did elect fellow founder Otto Wahrmund as vice-president, general manager of the brewery and acting president. This temporary leadership structure would not last long. The void at the top needed to be filled. As widow and sole beneficiary, Emma Koehler received all her husband's property and financial assets and, not long after, took control of San Antonio Brewing Association.

In 1915, San Antonio Brewing Association hired Otto Koehler's nephews, Charles and Otto Andrew Koehler. Charles came on as a clerk and would later become treasurer. Otto A. Koehler started as an assistant cashier, his first step toward what would later be the presidency of the organization.

From the time of Koehler's death until Prohibition was instituted, the San Antonio Brewing Association kept making beer, but it was in continual flux at the management level. Wahrmund remained interim president for a time, even after absentee co-founder and former SABA president Oscar Bergstrom came back into the picture. Bergstrom managed to get Emma Koehler's personal finance manager, Corwin T. Priest, appointed vice-president of SABA. The move was a shock to Emma Koehler, especially when Bergstrom later accused her of Priest's incompetence. It is likely that both the appointment and the recriminations were part of a campaign to wrest controlling interest in the brewery away from Koehler.

On April 6, 1914, U.S. senator Morris Sheppard of Texas introduced the Eighteenth Amendment to Congress. If passed, it would make all alcoholic beverages illegal. The nation's official first shot in the war on alcohol came the same day the United States officially entered World War I. Prohibition of alcohol in Texas was becoming more likely by 1915, and brewers and bar owners became increasingly worried about their future business prospects. Many bars had deals with breweries to sell their products exclusively, and Texas attorney general B.F. Looney filed an antitrust suit against Texas Brewers' Association, accusing it of creating a monopoly and conspiring against any Prohibition legislation. Not helping was the fact that the head of a Dallas brewery admitted that breweries had committed a percentage of their profits to anti-prohibition efforts. By 1917, San Antonio Brewing Association had disbanded its existing charter in favor of one that would form a corporation, thus shielding stockholders from any personal liability. Wahrmund was elected officially as president of the new board.

Also in 1917, Congress passed the Wartime Food and Fuel Act, prohibiting the use of grain for alcohol during wartime. A few months later, Texas governor William P. Hobby declared local prohibition in Texas. In September 1918, the federal government declared a "wartime" prohibition for the nation to start on July 1, 1919, even though the war had ended.

As if federal Prohibition weren't enough, the feds came after several San Antonio Brewing Association employees, including Priest, for tax evasion. Despite the charges, Priest was still elected as SABA president in 1919, after Wahrmund's resignation over a dispute with the board on the brewery's direction during Prohibition. Emma Koehler was elected vice-president, thus ushering in Pearl's third period. In contrast to Lone Star, whose leaders dissolved the company and closed the door on the brewery after the Volstead Act made Prohibition more than a temporary measure, SABA wanted to

An artist's rendering of the San Antonio Brewing Association after the new brewhouse and other buildings were added in the mid- to late 1890s. Seen are the stables, brewhouse, small train and various office buildings. *UTSA Libraries Special Collections.*

keep people working and a way to maintain the facilities in case it ever got to brew beer again.

In finding alternative businesses to stay afloat, San Antonio Brewing Association re-formed as Alamo Industries and later Alamo Food Company. The brewery changed its production to making various sodas and a near beer called La Perla. The ice plant was used to make ice for the locals, and the mechanical shop turned its attention to repairing cars for the city. Other buildings on the brewery grounds were used as a dry cleaners, cold storage and a dye plant. Spent grain left over from making the near beer was sold to area farmers as feed for their animals.

The enterprises kept things afloat, but hard times were made even harder when the stock market crashed in October 1929 and the Great Depression began. These deteriorating times forced several board members who were in great debt to sell their shares to Emma Koehler. Although Koehler kept her position as vice-president, she is largely credited for being the one with the determination and plans to keep the business going. Much like Eleanor

Roosevelt with President Franklin Roosevelt, Emma Koehler became the driving force behind San Antonio Brewing Association. Although her husband's death was tragic, it is possible that without that event, she never would have had her shot at running the show and steering it through the troubles ahead.

Her nephew Otto A. Koehler had been absent from the brewery and fighting the war in Europe. He returned to a home where Prohibition had stripped down the family business in which he had grown up. The young Koehler started several of his own businesses and stood by to help his aunt whenever she needed him.

Chapter 5

Pearl Brewery

1933-2001 and New Pearl

I n April 1933, with the Great Depression in full swing and a nation
desperate for jobs, including those provided by breweries and bars,
President Roosevelt signed a six-page document legalizing beer that
contained no more than 3.2 percent alcohol. It was the beginning of the end
for Prohibition, although Texas elected to remain dry.

In mid-1933, San Antonio Brewing Association returned to its original
name and started brewing beer again under a special permit to sock away
for maturation while a months-long battle ensued to also repeal Prohibition
in Texas. At the stroke of midnight on September 15, 1933, one hundred
trucks of beer rolled through the gates of the brewery to fill orders through
the city. Twenty-five boxcars of beer also went out on the little spur from
the brewery to link with locomotives standing by for deliveries throughout
the region. One photo from that day in 1933 shows cases of Pearl being
loaded onto a small airplane to get it quickly to some thirsty destination.
With no other breweries left in business in the region, everyone who
celebrated that day in much of Texas and the Southwest most likely did it
with a Pearl in hand.

By this time, Otto A. Koehler had returned to employment at San Antonio
Brewing Association as department head for its Orange Crush division,
returning the name Otto Koehler to the brewery's management. Emma
Koehler was finally named president of the organization in 1933, and Otto
became vice-president. She would keep that role until her death in 1943.
After that, Otto A. Koehler was elected by the board to serve as president

This montage of postcards illustrates several aspects of the Pearl Brewery.

of the association, ushering in the fourth period in Pearl's history. He would oversee unprecedented growth for the brewery until his death in 1969.

Otto Wahrmund, who returned to the brewery for a time in the 1920s, tried to help keep things in shape after staving off advances by Bergstrom to gain control of the company. By then, his health was poor, and he left the city for his ranch in Kerrville, where he died in 1929. Bergstrom, however, did manage to get an outside company to come in and manage the firm even as Emma Koehler tried everything she could to keep it going. The harsh management style of the outsiders caused trouble with the unions, and it took one of their hires, B.B. McGimsey, to restore relations with the workers.

Emma Koehler stands holding one of the first bottles of Pearl to come off the bottling line after Prohibition. Standing next to her is one of SABA's executives. *UTSA Libraries Special Collections, with permission of the* San Antonio Express-News.

McGimsey, who later became head of Pearl Brewing Company, was instrumental in bringing the brewery back into regional dominance once Prohibition was lifted and worked closely with first Emma and then Otto A. Koehler. McGimsey served two terms as head of San Antonio's chamber of commerce and was president the Texas Brewers Institute from its inception in 1935 until at least 1953. He left the brewery shortly after the expansion and went to found Kelly Field National Bank, which was an important financial institution in the city until it was later swallowed by larger banks in a period of consolidation.

Another stalwart who helped restart the brewery was Gustav Josef Etter. The brewer took over the brewing operations in 1904, stayed through Prohibition and brought the brewery back to life as beer was ready to flow once again. Etter, a native of Rottweil, Germany, had served as treasurer of the United States Brewers Association. He stayed with Pearl until his retirement in 1945. So beloved was he at the brewery and among his peers that a party put on by the brewery for his eighty-fifth birthday drew industry leaders from across the country.

Pearl's growing popularity in post-Prohibition years came partly from its sales and marketing ploys. Hyram "Pat" O'Brien devised the campaign

Pearl delivery truck, early twentieth century. *UTSA Libraries Special Collections.*

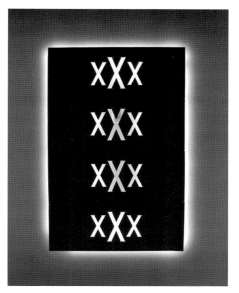

The XXX branding for SABA's Pearl beer harkens back to medieval days, when XXX meant the highest-quality beer. *Nan Palermo. Creative Commons attribution 2.0 generic license.*

declaring Pearl as coming from the "Country of 1100 Springs," a catchphrase that stuck long after Pearl had fallen out of favor with local drinkers. He also played up the Judge Roy Bean "Law West of the Pecos" legends in connection to Pearl since it had been said that it was the only beer he would serve in his bar and courtroom in the late 1800s. A replica of Bean's Jersey Lilly bar could be found at the back of the stage inside the Corral event venue that once housed the brewery's draft horses. The events center later became known as the Jersey Lilly. In its current form, the popular venue is known as the Pearl Stables. Also, thanks to O'Brien and Pearl publicist Aubrey Kline, Adolph Hofner's popular Texas Swing band became the Pearl Wranglers and created a strong bond between drinkers and the popular music of the time. Koehler, at O'Brien's retirement celebration in 1966, also credited the master of sales with building the distributor network from thirty-five to four hundred Pearl distributors in forty-two states.

The San Antonio Brewing Association took its place in the history books in 1952 when, after sixty-seven years, the board decided to change the name to align with the product for which it was best known: Pearl beer. Pearl Brewing Company came to be even as its last major expansion was underway.

In 1953, a special section in the *San Antonio Express* declared, "Pearl Now Largest Brewery in the Southwest." The expansion gave the newly renamed brewery 50 percent more capacity than previously to make 1.15 million barrels of beer annually. The new buildings also allowed room to add more equipment as needed. A massive beer storage area added fifty-seven glass tanks, each holding 880 barrels of Pearl on the first three floors. The fourth and fifth floors gave more space for fermentation. They also added a canning shop that could package six-packs or cases of Pearl at a rapid eighteen thousand cans per hour, with room for future expansion. The

The Pearl Brewery complex, circa 1950s. *UTSA Libraries Special Collections.*

improved bottling operations brought the number of bottling lines to four. The payroll that year hit $2.2 million, making it a formidable corporate citizen for its time.

The articles at the time of expansion also gave some insight into Otto A. Koehler, who had taken complete control of the brewery just ten years earlier, after his aunt's death. He had gone to the Wahl-Henius Brewmasters School in Chicago in 1934 to hone his technical skills. It was there that he was classmates with Harry Haeglin, who was brewmaster and plant manager at the time of the 1953 expansion of Pearl. It was also revealed that Koehler was not there for the expansion kickoff because he was in Africa and had recently killed the largest elephant seen in Kenya in the past fifteen years.

The next big move was an acquisition. In 1961, Pearl bought the Goetz Brewing Company of St. Joseph, Missouri. The two primary brands from that addition were Country Club Malt Liquor and Goetz Pale Near Beer.

Only a year after Koehler's death, the brewery was purchased by Southdown Inc., a company that had made its fortune in the sugar cane plantation and processing business early in the century but had been recently diversifying its portfolio for decades to become a conglomerate with soft drink, brewing, oil and gas, cement, vineyards and wineries, pistachio farms and candy production companies.

Only a year after Southdown bought the brewery and worried about slipping market share, Pearl went after two of its biggest competitors. While Pearl had been one of the largest beer purveyors in the state in 1953, its fortunes were changing even before Koehler's death. In 1971, Pearl went to court to stop Anheuser-Busch and Jos. Schlitz Brewing Company from engaging in what it alleged were illegal pricing schemes to take market share from Pearl in Texas. By 1970, A-B was by far the largest brewing company in America, selling more than 22 million barrels that year. A decade later, that figure would top 50 million barrels per year. Schlitz,

"From the Country of 1100 Springs," as it was known, Pearl's famous catchphrase was devised by Hyram "Pat" O'Brien. *Nan Palmero.*

too, was a company on the rise, going from 5.7 million barrels per year in 1960 to 15.1 million in 1970. Pearl alleged that the two companies were offering special discounts through their Texas distributors on certain beers so that retailers could sell them below or at the same prices as Pearl beers. That, argued Pearl lawyers, was essentially an anti-competitive way to get retailers to help them monopolize the market. Pearl wanted the practice stopped, but the U.S. District Court judge in Houston would not grant the request for relief in 1972.

Dissident Southdown shareholders eventually brought about a change in management at the company and began a massive divestiture of most of these businesses, including breweries, all the while beefing up the concrete and cement business. It was through that divestment that the company sold Pearl to Paul Kalmanovitz's San Francisco–based S&P Company in 1977.

With Kalmanovitz's tight grip on the purse strings, Pearl didn't have much of a marketing budget compared to Anheuser-Busch, Miller and Coors, but it knew how to work a gimmick. In October 1980, the brewery tied itself to the popularity of a television show called *Dallas*, whose lead character and villain was Texas ranch owner and oilman J.R. Ewing. In the March 1980 season finale, J.R. was shot, and the CBS network got a lot of mileage out of viewers trying to figure out "who shot J.R.?" from among his numerous enemies. The answer was revealed in a November 1980 episode. Nearly two months before that revelation, Pearl put out a beer called J.R. Ewing's Private Stock and sold about 1 million cases in a short time before orders slowed. "People buy an image, not a beer. This beer will do well for us as long as the television show does well," Pearl's director of marketing services Jack Kratz told the *New York Times* in mid-1981. But although the show was still on the air, orders had slowed, and only special orders were being filled on demand. "It just dropped off quickly as the interest in the situation in the TV program dropped off," Kratz told the *Times*. "Once they found out who shot the guy, it was over."

In 1981, Pearl had 535 employees and produced 1.8 million barrels of beer for forty-five states, although most was concentrated in Texas. As the portfolio of beers owned by Pearl's parent company grew, so did opportunities to brew more beers at the San Antonio facility. Kalmanovitz had been consolidating breweries for more than two decades, including gaining control of the powerhouse Falstaff Brewing (which had tried to force him to sell to it sixteen years earlier). When he bought the one-time major player Pabst Brewing Company in 1985, he shut down the Milwaukee brewery and headquarters of Pabst and moved the headquarters to the administration building at Pearl in San Antonio. That made the now San Antonio–based Pabst the fourth-largest brewing company in the nation.

Fortunes were changing, and by 1990, price pressures, competition and the portfolio of breweries Kalmanovitz had acquired over the years had become inefficient without upgrades. Even after the beer magnate's death in 1987, the trustees running the charitable trust in which he had placed all his assets weren't going to spend money on improvements. That led the company to ask Pearl workers who were members of the Teamsters Local 1110 to take a four-dollar-per-hour cut in pay to keep the brewery going. By 1995, the Pearl Brewery made only 1.1 million barrels of beer, returning it to the same level as forty years earlier and down nearly 40 percent from 1981.

Still, consolidation in the industry continued, and San Antonio's Pabst Brewing Company was doing much of the buying. In February 1999, Pabst acquired most of the brands of Detroit-based Stroh Brewing Company along with two of its breweries. The $405 million deal included giving up the Pabst-owned Old English 800 brand, then the bestselling malt liquor in the country, to Miller Brewing Company in exchange for help in financing the deal. Pabst picked up eleven brands, including iconic regional brands like Chicago-born Old Style, the Pacific Northwest's Ranier and Olympia and the once San Antonio–made Lone Star. Other brands in the deal included former national rival Schlitz and Hamm's.

In June 1999, Pabst Brewing Company brought production of Lone Star back to San Antonio and rolled its first cans and bottles of Lone Star out of the Pearl Brewery to great fanfare. With "Certified Brewed in San Antonio" on the label, Lone Star sales rose 17 percent. It was free media and goodwill for a brand that San Antonians had once adored. By that time, Pabst had sold its Lehigh Valley plant in Pennsylvania and sold off the former Olympia Brewery in Washington to Miller. That left only Pearl still brewing brands owned by parent Pabst. All others were contract-brewed at various Miller Brewing Company plants around the country.

Less than a year after Pearl started making Lone Star in San Antonio again, Pabst Brewing Company officials announced that they would be closing Pearl Brewery. It was the beginning of the ten-day Fiesta celebration and just before Easter Sunday, generally a time of great celebration in San Antonio, when the announcement came down that San Antonio's largest and oldest surviving brewery would be no more. Pabst officials said the closure meant that more than three hundred workers would lose their jobs on June 30, 2000.

Union members at Pearl offered to management that they would take a two-year freeze of benefits and wages if it would help keep the brewery open. The offer was rejected. "The wage and benefit freeze is a nice gesture, but that isn't going to do it," Pabst CEO Bill Bitting told the *San Antonio Express-News*. On April 27, union leaders once again met with Pabst management to delay the planned closure. Once again, the company CEO, S&P trustee and San Francisco–based lawyer Bitting rejected the notion of trying to save the San Antonio jobs. "It's just too costly to keep it open," he said. Production of Pearl, Lone Star, Pabst, Schlitz, Old Milwaukee, Colt 45 malt liquor and the company's other beers were destined to be brewed under contract by the massive and modern Miller Brewing Company plant in Fort Worth. Regional brands owned by Pabst in other parts of the country were already made at Miller breweries in those regions at a fraction of the overhead cost of brewing them in-house.

Brewing was so ingrained in the consciousness of the San Antonio community that it was hard to let go, and union officials challenged the decision again. Pearl employee David Mahaffey was defiant, at the time saying, "Until the last day we're producing a product, we'll put out the best quality we can because we take pride in our jobs. We make the best beer in the world right here. We want to keep the place open." In early May, the Teamsters Local 1110 made an undefined offer to purchase from Pabst the brewery along with the Pearl and Lone Star brands. It planned to use money from the national union, pension plan funds and conventional financing. "The beer consumers of San Antonio will not drink these brands [Pearl and Lone Star] if they are brewed elsewhere," said union business manager George Eichler.

By mid-May, Pabst managers had hammered out a deal with the teamsters to keep the Pearl Brewery open for at least another three years, albeit with fewer than 50 employees and production of fewer than 500,000 barrels of beer per year, focusing just on the native Pearl and Lone Star brands. On June 30, more than 260 Pearl brewers and support staff were checked out by guards at the gate to make sure they hadn't taken a last memento with them from the property. On their last day, they sat on the open tailgates of their pickup trucks, sipped on tallboys of Lone Star and swapped stories with one another and one of this book's authors, who was reporting the story for the *San Antonio Express-News*. "This is a beautiful place to work and beautiful people," said George Bialas, a sixty-two-year-old forklift operator. But "a lot of people bought cars, homes. Why did they have to do this to us?"

After the first round of layoffs, Pabst officials told the last eighty brewery workers that all remaining production would move to a Miller plant in late April 2001. The three-year deal with the union was no more, and the 115-year-old brewery, with its struggles and triumphs, became part of the city's history instead of the living institution it had been.

Pabst Brewing Company maintained its headquarters in the former Pearl administration building for a few years more, but a later CEO of the company never took to San Antonio and moved headquarters closer to his Chicago home, citing the city's ties to the Old Style brand, long out of fashion, as the reason for the move. The company went through several CEOs until a Greek turnaround magnate bought Pabst and turned it over to his sons in Beverly Hills. The firm is now owned by a Russian American with capital from a Russian investor. While there has been some talk about returning some of these brands to their roots, the company hasn't made public any plans to bring the Pearl or Lone Star brands back to San Antonio production. Pearl is still made, but in small quantities, while Lone Star has maintained popularity among the young and old in San Antonio and beyond thanks to the bargain-basement prices and the old-school cachet it still carries.

The brewery grounds are now a mixed-use development that pays homage to the history of the place. Christopher "Kit" Goldsbury's Silver Ventures bought the property in 2002 at a bargain and has invested considerable sums into a slow and thoughtful restoration and development of the space. It now houses numerous companies, nonprofit organizations, a host of eclectic restaurants, apartments, shops, a bookstore and the nation's third campus of the Culinary Institute of America. In recent years, the house once belonging to the Pearl Brewery's cooper (who made beer barrels for the brewery) has been transformed to the Granary 'Cue & Brew, bringing house-made beer back to the Pearl. Inside the former brewhouse building, Southerleigh Fine Food & Brewery has taken root and brought national attention to the historic site, with beer once again flowing from the classic brewery.

Chapter 6

Lone Star

Lone Star is best known today for its advertising slogan "The National Beer of Texas," recalling a time that Texas was its own nation after freeing itself from Mexican rule. But the first Lone Star brewery didn't come along until nearly forty years after Texas statehood, and there wasn't even a beer called Lone Star until twenty years after the original brewery permanently closed thanks to Prohibition.

The Lone Star story can be a confusing one, thanks in part to the acquisitive nature of its founder, the famed St. Louis brewery owner Adolphus Busch. Busch, who with his father-in-law formed St. Louis's Anheuser-Busch Brewing Company, decided to branch out beyond the company and invest or launch breweries in other states. To that end, he teamed up with John Hermann Kampmann, the man responsible for building many of the structures that defined San Antonio in the latter half of the nineteenth century, and several other San Antonio businessmen to form Lone Star Brewery. Louis Kalteyer and Louis Berg were two other San Antonians linked to the brewery.

Kampmann, who had built the home of longtime San Antonio brewer Charles Degen and overseen construction of the Menger Hotel on top of the Western Brewery, led a meeting of five other local businessmen and tradesmen on August 6, 1883, at Fire Station No. 2. At that meeting, he raised about $85,000 of the $100,000 needed to start Lone Star Brewing Association. He then teamed up with Busch and Edward Hoppe. They formed a mutual stock company, and Kampmann was named the first president. But Busch was the one with expertise in designing and running

Opened in 1981 after a multimillion-dollar renovation, the San Antonio Museum of Art now occupies the old Lone Star Brewing Company brewhouse near San Antonio's downtown.

breweries and took the lead on much of the process thereafter. Kampmann's son, Hermann, was treasurer of the group in 1884 and took over duties as president after his father's death in 1885.

In St. Louis, Busch had met the young and ambitious Otto Koehler working in an administrative position at a competing brewery in the city. He recruited Koehler to manage the new operation in San Antonio, which launched in 1884. This was done in part through an acquisition of William Esser's brewery and Lone Star Bottling assets in San Antonio. At that point, Anheuser-Busch was already sending its beer by rail from St. Louis to San Antonio and other metropolitan areas around the country. Koehler's task was to manage a brewery making beer different than that of Anheuser-Busch so it could capture revenue from a crowd that wanted to drink local. He did the same with breweries in Houston, Galveston and Dallas.

When the brewery was finished in 1884, the cost was $150,000, but it was the most mechanized brewery in Texas at the time. Just two years later, Koehler borrowed money from his brother-in-law to invest in the competing San Antonio Brewing Association and took an unauthorized trip to Germany, which is when he probably acquired the recipe and rights to what would become SABA's signature Pearl beer. By 1886, he was managing

A. A. BUSCH, Prest.   PHIL. CARL, Vice Prest. and Gen'l Mgr.

Lone Star Brewing Company.

STANDARD AND PELSENER BEERS

Unexcelled by Any Brand in The Market.

BOTTLING A SPECIALTY.   Telephone No. 13.

JONES AVE., San Antonio, Texas.

Lone Star Brewing Company, "Unexcelled by Any Brand in the Market." It seems that everyone's beer was the best brew out there. *From Street, Avenue and Alley Guide to San Antonio, Texas, edited by Jules A. Appler, 1892. City of San Antonio.*

the new enterprise, but correspondence shows that he was still in touch with Busch, whom he saw as a mentor in the brewing business.

The new brewery was met with great fanfare, drawing two thousand or more visitors to hear speeches, the Eighth Cavalry Band and the Fashion Theater Band and see a parade of employees marching around downtown with a massive keg of beer.

Eight years after Lone Star opened, Busch bought out the partners in the venture and owned it outright. He then made a major investment in the brewery, replacing wood-framed buildings with brick structures and adding capacity to become one of the biggest breweries in the state. Production eventually hit sixty-five thousand barrels per year, but wartime rationing of ingredients used in beer and then Prohibition caused Lone Star to close up shop. It tried making a soft drink called Tango and operating as an ice company before closing for good. For decades, the buildings were used by various businesses as warehouse space or storage, In the 1970s, the San Antonio Museum of Art bought the building and began to convert it to the new museum, which opened in 1981.

The second era for Lone Star was in name only. Just two weeks before the ban on beer was lifted in 1933, Champion Brewing Company started construction on a new brewery just south of downtown off Mission Road on land believed to be a training ground for Teddy Roosevelt and his Rough Riders in the late 1890s. Champion was completed and brewing beers under the Champion and Sabinas names by the dawn of 1935.

Right: An old vestige of Lone Star's past, this emblem still adorns the building now occupied by the San Antonio Museum of Art.

Below: The second iteration of the Lone Star Brewing Company had the latest brewing equipment and processes and treated employees to a well-landscaped campus that included a small lake. *UTSA Libraries Special Collections*.

Peter Kreil, a brewer from Munich, changed the name of Champion Brewery in 1940 to Lone Star Brewing Company, taking a page from the city's pre-Prohibition past. He also formulated the first beer to bear the name Lone Star and was making thirty-nine thousand barrels of lager over the next year. Because the brewery became an instant landmark for that part of town, the public road leading to the brewery is called Lone Star Boulevard.

In 1949, under the leadership of Lone Star president Harry Jersig, the company did a public offering of stock and became the first San Antonio brewery with shares on the stock exchange.

Lone Star decided in 1956 that it was ready to make the brewery a destination where people could come for a few beers. What turned it into the greatest tasting room in brewery history was the purchase of the Buckhorn bar, a downtown saloon opened in 1881 by Albert Friedrich, a one-time bellhop and barman at the hotel across the street from the building that was to become his saloon. Buckhorn became a favorite watering hole for locals and dusty, trail-worn travelers. Seeing that many didn't have money, he began accepting animal horns or racks of antlers in exchange for a beer or whiskey. The collection grew over the years to cover walls and ceilings. When Prohibition shut down his alcohol sales at the saloon, he used his much-talked-about collection of horns and other strange finds gathered over the years to draw in visitors for lunches, sodas and other non-alcoholic beverages.

Friedrich kept collecting and even paid one traveler $100 for a seventy-eight-point buck rack. He may have thrown in a few beers for good measure for such a find. Hundreds of stuffed animal species are represented in the collection, including one bovine that died from a horn growing into its eye and into the brain. His wife, Emile, also decided to start collecting and would give a drink for a jar of rattlesnake rattlers, which she would then turn into elaborate, framed artworks.

When Lone Star bought it from the family, the structure was moved to 600 Lone Star Boulevard and placed in a special building constructed next to the brewery to house the bar and all its attendant oddities. The collection continued to grow at Lone Star and was a family favorite and tourist attraction until the last owners of the brewery decided to shut down the brewery and any amusements on the property. Albert Friedrich's granddaughter Mary Friedrich Rogers and her husband, Wallace, stepped in and bought the collection along with the rights to keep it on the defunct brewery property. They still brought in about 150,000 visitors per year but eventually helped form the Buckhorn Saloon and Museum downtown at East Houston and

Dusk sets over Alamo Beer with a serene view of the Alamo City from the historic Hays Street Bridge. Seen in the foreground is the brewery's office, beer garden and brewhouse. *Jeremy Banas.*

The calm before the storm. Mad Pecker Brewing Company gets ready to open its doors to serve its approximately twenty taps. The brewpub will soon have its own brews on tap. *Jeremy Banas.*

Thirsty patrons of Southtown staple the Friendly Spot wait for their chance to order one of dozens of craft beer options not available even seven years ago. *Jeremy Banas*.

The Menger Hotel in the early morning hours, once the site of San Antonio's (and arguably the state's) first licensed commercial brewery. *Menger Hotel*.

Seen from its zen-like courtyard, Southerleigh Fine Food & Brewery is only the second tenant of this historic brewhouse, completed in 1894. *Nan Palmero.*

Ranger Creek's tasting room is adorned with barrels filled with various ales for future release. Many of these barrels are devoted to its sour program. *Jeremy Banas.*

One of Big Hops' original employees, Aug Aranda is hard at work filling growlers (sixty-four-ounce vessels used for taking beer to go) for thirsty San Antonio patrons. *Jeremy Banas.*

With kegs of Freetail Beer loaded and ready for distribution to area stores, it's a historic time for the local brewery. *Nan Palmero*.

Lit up like rays of sunshine, beers from the Granary 'Cue & Brew's lineup sit waiting to be enjoyed alongside chef-prepared barbecue with a Texas- and world-cuisine flair. *Granary 'Cue & Brew*.

A fixture in Southtown, Blue Star Brewing is the center of First Friday events at the Blue Star Arts Complex, which sees thousands of attendees each month. *Blue Star Brewing Company.*

Raising a glass of Blue Star brew, owner and head brewer Joey Villarreal has been key in the resurgence of San Antonio's beer scene since 1994. Where's your brewer beard, Joey? *Blue Star Brewing Company.*

Still towering after all these years, one of Lone Star's smokestacks serves as reminder of glory days gone by. *Marc Toppel, Creative Commons Attribution 2.0 Generic, https://www.flickr.com/photos/marctoppel/4042443329/sizes/n.*

Busted Sandal taps are at the ready for the day's taproom hours. Busted Sandal is hidden away near San Antonio's Medical Center. *Jeremy Banas.*

Patrons at San Antonio's oldest surviving brewpub can sit less than six feet from the gleaming serving tanks behind the bar. *Blue Star Brewing Company.*

Once housing horses for Pearl's distribution around San Antonio, the stables have been used as storage, a bar and now an event center. *Nan Palmero.*

Cured restaurant at the new Pearl complex is sitting pretty at night. This building, completed in 1904, once housed the Pearl business offices. *Nan Palmero.*

Putting on his best hooligan face, soccer fan and Freetail founder Scott Metzger has spent much of his time fighting for brewery rights at the state level and serves on the board of directors for the national Brewers Association. *Nan Palmero.*

Sitting next to its brewing equipment is Ranger Creek Brewing and Distilling's magical "still," the tool of its award-winning distiller, T.J. Miller. *Jeremy Banas.*

Pints of Freetail's Rye Wit sit sunning themselves on the covered porch of Freetail's brewpub located off 1604 near Military Drive. *Nan Palmero.*

Right: Pearl XXX lager magazine ad. *Library of Congress, Prints & Photographs Division, photograph by Carol M. Highsmith.*

Below: A grain silo from Pearl's past sits in the courtyard of Southerleigh Fine Food & Brewery. Southerleigh plans to convert the silo into an intimate dining area. *Nan Palmero.*

Another reminder of Pearl's past sits atop the building now occupied by a local bike shop, another way that Silver Ventures has paid homage to the past while moving forward into the future. *Jeremy Banas.*

Several glasses from Boerne Brewery are ready and waiting for a tap takeover at craft beer and food truck destination Random. *Boerne Brewery.*

Frio lager still pulls on the heartstrings of some San Antonio residents, who remember the full-flavored lager and its pioneering owner/brewer, David Strain. *David Strain.*

A neon Lone Star bar sign. *Library of Congress, Prints & Photographs Division, photograph by Carol M. Highsmith.*

Above: A Lone Star magazine ad. *Library of Congress, Prints & Photographs Division, photograph by Carol M. Highsmith.*

Right: "The National Beer of Texas." Lone Star's second incarnation is still wildly popular among Texas residents, who still identify the former brewery with the Lone Star State. *Library of Congress, Prints & Photographs Division, photograph by Carol M. Highsmith.*

LONE STAR!

Above: A contemporary artist's rendering of a San Antonio resident enjoying Lone Star. *Mike "Dakinewavamon" Kline, Creative Commons Attribution 2.0 Generic, https://www.flickr.com/photos/mikekline/2678856030/sizes/o.*

Left: Adorning the wall of an unknown bar, this neon reminder of Lone Star's second incarnation is still a favorite of Texas residents. *Library of Congress, Prints & Photographs Division, photograph by Carol M. Highsmith.*

Above: Finally brewed at its own place, a mug of Alamo Golden Ale sits quietly next to an Alamo amber lager. *Nan Palmero.*

Below: At one of many events that Alamo Beer president Eugene Simor attends each week, the bottles and coasters are a reminder of the brewery's first logo incarnation during the days when it was brewed up at Real Ale. *Nan Palmero.*

Presa Streets, just a few blocks from the Alamo, where it remains a popular attraction and event space.

Lone Star's popularity continued to grow, even as Pearl was growing its business across town. In 1965, Lone Star production hit 1 million barrels for the year.

Brewery owner and manager Harry Jersig found himself competing not just with the neighboring Pearl but also with the ever-growing presence of Anheuser-Busch, Miller and Schlitz in the Texas market. He brought in Barry Sullivan from New England's Narragansett Brewing in 1973 to keep the "Texas is a Lone Star beer" state of mind. Sullivan went after the musicians and music lovers in the state, with a heavy focus on Austin's burgeoning new music scene. Free beer for acts at Austin's Armadillo World Headquarters got the attention of fans, and it got Sullivan a host of short jingles plugging Lone Star. When Armadillo World Headquarters and public television gave birth to the nationally broadcast *Austin City Limits* music television program, Lone Star was there as a sponsor to further its branding as the National Beer of Texas. Advertisements featuring armadillos and quirky Texas behavior

Eventually upgraded as a destination brewery for area residents and visitors, the second incarnation of Lone Star Brewing boasted a lake and handsome grounds. *Courtesy of UTSA Libraries Special Collections.*

cemented the brand, and by 1974, sales had increased by 1 million cases. Those armadillos would later figure into future radio, print and television ads in the 1980s under new ownership.

The brewery changed ownership five times in twenty years, beginning in 1976 with an acquisition by Olympia Brewing Company of Tumwater, Washington. Under Olympia's ownership, the brand didn't soar, but it was still big for a regional player, producing 1.5 million barrels of Lone Star, Lone Star Light and Buckhorn beer in 1981.

In 1983, G. Heileman Brewing of Wisconsin bought Olympia and gained the Lone Star brands and brewery in the deal. It held on to the brand for a decade trying to build the business with the whimsical advertisement featuring a giant armadillo attacking truckloads of Lone Star beer to make off with the goods. A leveraged buyout firm in Dallas called Hicks, Muse, Tate & Furst took ownership of the brewery in its 1993 purchase of G. Heileman, but it didn't hang on to it for long.

Detroit's Stroh Brewing Company, which had been accumulating budget beer brands for the past few years, bought the brewing firm from Hicks, Tate in 1996. Instead of putting much-needed capital into the brewery to modernize it and increase production, Stroh announced that it would close the Lone Star brewery, lay off more than five hundred employees at the end of September and move production to another brewery in the East Texas city of Longview. Representatives of the workers tried to convince Stroh to change its mind, but Stroh CEO William Henry said that it would cost more than $40 million to make needed improvements to the sixty-three-year-old brewery. The brand's value and potential in the marketplace just wasn't enough to justify that expenditure. Asked about the move of the brand from San Antonio to Longview, a downtown bar patron told the *San Antonio Express-News*, "It's like moving the Alamo to Odessa."

The newspaper reported that on the day the brewery closed, the strains of "Auld Lang Syne" echoed through the dark brewery as employees told one another goodbye and then quietly drove away.

It didn't do Longview much good either. In 1999, San Antonio–based Pabst bought most of the Stroh brands and some of its brewery assets. It closed the Longview plant and moved Lone Star back to San Antonio, where it was brewed for a short time in 2000 and part of 2001 at Pearl. Soon after, Pabst shuttered all of its breweries. The Lone Star brand is still owned by Pabst, and it is still made in Texas—this time under a contract by the massive MillerCoors brewery in Forth Worth.

The former brewery and property at 600 Lone Star Boulevard has changed hands several times over the years, but planned projects never came to fruition. The newest owner, AquaLand Development, bought the property in May 2015 and said that it wants to turn it into a mixed-use development over sixty acres that could include a microbrewery, a theater, a live-music venue, restaurants, loft apartments, retail and office space and parks. "Restoring a landmark like the Lone Star Brewery property is an expensive proposition," said AquaLand president Mark Smith. "We are hopeful that we can return most of the iconic features of the site to their former glory. I swam in the pool, played at the lake and sat with my grandfather in the beer garden overlooking the Buckhorn Saloon as a kid. We are going to work diligently with the city, state and others to restore as much of the site as economically feasible."

Chapter 7

The New Brew

1993-2008

The nation's brewing revolution was born in quiet desperation as those who dreamed of opening their own breweries knew that they would have to go big or go home to have a chance at making it. Instead, they just kept homebrewing and drinking whatever they could find with more flavor than what was produced by a handful of breweries across the country. Mostly what they found were imported beers in classic styles. In 1983, California laws were modernized to allow for brewpubs, and the innovation began. Brewpubs could be profitable because they could make beer in fairly small batches and sell directly to the consumer at the pub, which usually doubled as a restaurant.

It wasn't until 1993 that the Texas legislature got on board and allowed for brewpub licenses. The growth of the brewing industry in the state had been hampered by sixty-year-old alcohol legislation and a three-tier system that put a middleman distributor or wholesaler between the producer of the beer and the restaurant, bar or retailer where it was purchased. One of the primary reasons for the law was to prohibit "tied houses" that, prior to Prohibition, had sold the beer of only one brewery. In some parts of the country, it wasn't unusual for larger breweries to directly own chains of saloons and taverns.

Because most breweries without reserve capital couldn't return to business after Prohibition ended, only the largest and best-funded players returned to the marketplace, and the brewpub-like businesses, like those of Menger and Degen in the 1800s, were no longer legal. By the late 1980s, few brewing companies existed in the state or the nation. Consolidation meant that most domestically produced beers found in a San Antonio bar were made by Anheuser-Busch, Miller Brewing Company, Coors Brewing Company, Lone Star owner G. Heileman Brewing Company, Pearl owner Pabst Brewing Company or Stroh Brewing Company.

The tastes of the nation had changed in the last four generations as beer diversity dwindled. Those who had a taste for imported beers from England, Germany and Belgium or who had on their travels reveled in a fresh pint from a brewery such as San Francisco's pioneering Anchor Brewing Company wanted something more from their beer. The brewpub law in Texas opened up opportunities for existing restaurant owners to add brewing to their business and legitimized some who had already been brewing.

The first in San Antonio to take advantage of this was Boardwalk Bistro on Broadway, already a city staple and well known for its award-winning wine selection. Owner Randy Hunt jumped on this chance to fulfill his longtime passion for brewing. By the spring of 1994, Hunt, Blake Smithson and Warren Windsor had put four house beers on tap: a Vienna-style lager, a traditional German-style bock, an Irish-style stout and a tap that changed from week to week.

Adam Brogley was hired as head brewer for Boardwalk Bistro in February 1995 and employed traditional methods to make each beer as authentic to the style as possible. The restaurant is still going strong and continues to carry a diverse beer selection, but the brewing operation closed in the spring of 1997. Brogley went to brew at the Laboratory Brewing Company and then at Blue Star Brewing Company, where he was still making classic styles as of late 2015.

The year 1994 also brought San Antonio's first two microbrewery openings since before Prohibition. Frio Brewing Company and then Yellow Rose Brewing Company both put their beer out for public consumption to a San Antonio public that wasn't quite sure what to make of these flavorful creations. Unlike establishments with brewpub licenses, the Texas microbrewery laws of the time didn't allow direct sales to the consumer, but they could get their beer sold in more places by self-distribution or through a distributor.

Frio Brewing began as an extension of one man's passion. David Strain was working in the space industry as an engineer for Southwest Research Institute in the early 1990s when his homebrewing hobby began to evolve into plans for opening his own brewery. "Some of the guys I worked with were brewing their own beer at home, and that kind of brought out the bug in me," said Strain, who credited an unlikely source for actually inspiring him to start brewing at home. "I had come across an article in an issue of Martha Stewart's magazine that discussed making a sourdough starter with various fruit added. Somehow in making it myself, the smell of the yeast really hit home, and I decided it was time to jump into homebrewing."

Soon after Strain bought his equipment, he set up a large outdoor cooler to use as a controlled fermentation space and began brewing. Not wanting to pull himself in too many directions, he decided to focus on just one beer to start off Frio. "We just wanted to be really good at one beer. Often breweries can overextend themselves with too many mediocre styles. We wanted one really good one," Strain said. Fascinated with Boston Beer Company's Samuel Adams Boston Lager, Strain focused his take on that style to become Frio Lager Beer. He wanted to honor San Antonio's lager brewing past, as well as meet the requirements of the city's taste for crisp and refreshing beers. With that in mind, he brewed his lager over and over until he was happy with the finished product.

Knowing that he planned to open a brewery, Strain purchased the building at 1905 North St. Mary's Street for a bargain price of $93,000. The building had at one point served as the Nehi bottling plant for the San Antonio area. Strain figured that if his brewery didn't materialize, he could later flip it for a profit. With a business plan, a beer and a brewhouse design in hand, Strain managed to wrangle thirty-six investors for $1.2 million to start the operation. "Back then, it was just my wife, Pam, and I doing this. I remember going to Kinko's to print out the labels we'd designed and then gluing them to the bottles so that we had something to show the investors," Strain recalled.

Strain took his brewery seriously, becoming inspired by the likes of small-brewery advocate Charlie Papazian, a homebrewing guru and Brewers Association founder. David and Pam Strain began attending brewing industry events to get the lay of the land, meet with equipment manufacturers and ingredient suppliers and exchanging ideas with other fledgling beer entrepreneurs such as Kim Jordan of New Belgium Brewing Company.

Harnessing his experience as a mechanical engineer, Strain designed his brewery with a 30-barrel brewhouse, 60-barrel fermentation tanks and 120-barrel aging tanks then custom manufactured by AAA Fabrication. A used sixty-head bottle filler was refurbished by John Visel, who was working on a similar system in Oregon at Deschutes Brewing. Visel died before the project was completed, but his son stepped in and finished the job to help bring Frio to life.

Strain brought in brewer Larry Cash to assist in the installation of the equipment and to make the brewing process as efficient as possible, with a goal to keep each step of the brewing process to no more than an hour. David Owers was added to the brewing staff and used his mechanical skills to keep the operation running smoothly.

Once a month, the brewery hosted Frio Friday, with live music, informal tours and free Frio lager. The now internationally known Two Tons of Steel rockabilly band was a regular at the event, which became popular with locals. The beer caught the attention of several people with their own dreams of opening breweries, including Joey Villarreal, who was brewing small batches of beer at his bar just down the street from Frio and would later open Blue Star Brewing Company.

The popularity of the free events and the eye-catching labels featuring a green gecko ultimately didn't translate into enough beer sales to balance the books. In those days, it was hard to convince a bar to bump even a duplicative Bud Light tap for an untried local beer, and getting limited space in the grocery store beer cooler also proved difficult. It wasn't until several years in that the brand was extended with the addition of Frio Honey Wheat, which did reach additional drinkers who were not fans of the original lager.

A mural painted by Robert Tatum is what little remains externally of Frio Brewing Company, which opened in 1994 and was San Antonio's first new production brewery to open since Prohibition. *Travis E. Poling.*

As debts mounted, Strain said that he felt abandoned by his distributors and went through three wholesalers in the five years of operation. Strain also alleged that instances of sabotage by competitors were not uncommon, including cutting the handles on Frio six-pack holders at some stores, causing the bottles to fall out when the carton was picked up. The brewery closed in 1999, even as new breweries were starting to find their footing in the market.

The former brewery property was purchased by San Antonio–

based Gambrinus Company, which owns the Spoetzl Brewery and its Shiner brands along with several other breweries and brands around the country. The now-faded murals by artist Robert Tatum can still be seen by passersby, and over the years, Gambrinus has used the brewery for test batches (although not of Shiner beers) and, more recently, for hand-mixing variety twelve-packs of beer for stores such as Costco and Sam's.

History has shown that Frio was ahead of its time, but it served to inspire others to open their own breweries. Strain, who now runs a popular restaurant with his wife, said that he takes comfort in that.

Shortly after Frio opened its doors, homebrewer and oral surgeon Glen A. Fritz launched his small-batch microbrewery, Yellow Rose Brewing Company. The brewery was named for the famed "Yellow Rose of Texas," the legend of a young woman who distracted Mexican general Antonio Lopez de Santa Anna with her feminine wiles long enough for Texan liberation forces to rout the Mexican army. Legends like this made up the backbone of the brewery's branding strategy, with whimsical, sometimes made-up tall tales gracing the labels of the twenty-two-ounce bottles.

Yellow Rose brands didn't have much of a presence in the draft market, but even at a capacity of about 2,400 barrels per year, it managed to have a fairly wide distribution around the state with its bottles. The ales included Blond Ox, Bubba Dog (an American-style wheat beer), Cactus Queen, Honcho Grande Brown Ale, Yellow Rose Pale Ale, Vigilante Porter and Wildcatter's Crude Stout, which was later renamed Wildcatter's Refined Stout.

Early on, the brewery began to win awards with brewers like Jason Courtney, who later went on to win even more prestigious awards with Hub City brewpub in Lubbock. Other brewers during its six-year run included Starr Center, former Frio brewer Larry Cash and Ray Mitteldorf, who has since helmed the brewing operations at three Texas brewpubs in Houston and the San Antonio area.

For the most part, it was a family affair, with even Fritz's parents helping out on bottling days. But even as the craft beer scene in Texas was showing some signs of staying power, family members weren't interested in continuing the operation, and it closed in the summer of 2000.

While Yellow Rose is still remembered fondly in San Antonio beer aficionado circles, it ended up with a black mark on its name that had nothing to do with the beer produced by the brewery in San Antonio. A Dallas company called Great Grains bought the rights to the Yellow Rose brands, the recipes and the leftover labels. Until 2005, when Great Grains was shut down by the Texas Alcoholic Beverage Commission, it produced infected versions of the beer at its Dallas brewery using the same labels proclaiming it was made in San Antonio.

In 1995, housed in a renovated 1898 feed and grocery store, North St. Mary's Brewing Company began brewing its own beer and also had one of the largest bottle and tap selections in town with forty-five taps and fifty in bottles ranging from imports to the nascent craft breweries of the West Coast. But by 1997, brewing had ceased, and it functioned as a beer bar and live music venue until arson turned it to ashes in September 2000.

One brewery that did have staying power is the brewpub Blue Start Brewing Company, which over the last twenty years has become a mainstay of modern brewing consciousness of the city. Inspired by Frio, Yellow Rose and his own brewing experiments at his neighborhood bar Joey's, Joey Villarreal and his wife, Maggie, built Blue Star Brewing Company in the Blue Star Arts Complex, now a thriving center for the arts, dining and night life in a former warehouse district next to the historic King William residential area just south of the hubbub of downtown.

As a bar owner, Villarreal couldn't open a microbrewery, so in 1996, he decided that the new (to Texas) brewpub concept was the way to go. Villarreal always had a passion for beer, but he knew that opening a new business could be risky. He had read a few publications about brewpubs, and after having made a trip to Great Lakes Brewing Company in Ohio, he took the leap of opening Blue Star. Villarreal was also inspired by California beer staple Sierra Nevada, prompting him to look to the University of California–Davis and its heralded brewing program to get him on track. Villarreal then looked to consulting brewer Charlie Jordan and University of Texas–San Antonio fermentation science professor Dr. Paul Farnsworth for additional guidance.

Farnsworth also helped make Villarreal's cask ale the first successfully brewed in modern Texas. Cask ales are beers that have been aged in barrels for an additional period of time, sometimes with additional adjuncts added for character. Because they use only a low level of natural carbonation, Blue Star installed the city's first hand-pumped beer engine to pull the beer out for serving.

Unlike many who jumped into the brewpub and microbrewery scene in the early days, Villarreal had experience in the food service and alcoholic beverage business, cutting his teeth with Joey's, a bar with a laid-back feel and still a local fixture. In fact, it was at Joey's that Villarreal began brewing small batches of beer with brewer Charlie Jordan, testing them out on his patrons.

Villarreal described his approach to the brewpub as wanting to create as friendly an atmosphere as possible, much like the bar. With having seen many wineries get into trouble due to a belief that they were pretentious, he wanted to give the patrons at Blue Star a feeling of not having to worry about whether a beer was a pale ale or a lager—only that it's beer. If folks want to know more, he is more than happy to oblige with more information about that particular beer. "You are only as good as your last beer, after all," he said.

When opening Blue Star, Villarreal picked a location in an old beer storage warehouse, and the brewpub's décor maintains much of that original look. He also helped fuel the biking culture in the area and opened Blue Star Bike Shop inside the pub, although it is now a freestanding business next door between the pub and his new intimate music venue and bar Joe Blues. Many organized bicycle rides begin and end in the Blue Star parking lot, with thirsty cyclists stopping in for a pint after a ride.

Blue Star experimented with many styles in the early years, but after a while, he decided that it was easier to just keep it simple, focusing on perfecting basic styles with an emphasis on classic European ales and lagers. Typical offerings include a pale ale, a light Mexican-style lager called Texican, Spire Stout, a wheat beer dubbed Wheathead, the signature winter brew King William barleywine and sour beers in several varieties, including the tart and fruity Raspberry Geyser. India pale ale, English mild, pilsner and a smoky ale called Smoked Dark also make occasional appearances on tap.

Beer guru Michael Jackson, known for his widely popular show *Beer Hunter* and numerous books on the world's favorite fermented beverage, came to San Antonio and praised Blue Star's Spire Stout. In 2000, he was back in the city and gave compliments to Blue Star's Euro Pils, which is no longer part of the lineup.

The kitchen at Blue Star has gone through many changes over the years, from typical pub fare to a high-end gastropub menu. The latest incarnation walks the line between the two concepts, using locally sourced and organic ingredients as much as possible. Sodas brewed on site use natural cane sugar, and the beer has gone organic.

The same year Blue Star made its entrance, the Laboratory Brewing Company opened in the laboratory building of the former Alamo Cement plant. A massive upscale retail and entertainment complex called Alamo Quarry Market was built in and around the imposing remnants of the plant just across the street from the brewpub.

The Laboratory's steady offerings include Concrete Blonde and Javelina Hefe hefeweizen. Available on a rotating basis were Alamo Amber Ale, San Jose Brown Ale, Coal Porter, Yellow Dog Pale Ale and a strong Calibration Ale.

Joe Barfield, who had worked at Colorado's Tabernash Brewing, was the first brewer and served as general manager of the Lab, as it was commonly known. It was open for lunch and dinner but became a nightlife hot spot for the younger crowd, with weekly swing dance lessons. Adam Brogley, the former Boardwalk Bistro brewer, came on board to take over beer-making duties until a management shakeup. Jason Davis, a seasoned brewer from his time at two Austin breweries, was the last brewer before the owners sold the Lab in 2002. The space has housed a succession of short-lived restaurants until it found a steady tenant with the beer-centric restaurant Quarry Hofbrau.

In New Braunfels, a drought of locally made beer was lifted when, in 1998, the owners of the historic Faust Hotel opened a brewpub inside its bar and restaurant. Faust Brewing Company went through several brewers before it sold a drop of beer, and a succession of brewers followed, with some making only one or two batches on the system before moving on.

Brewing operations eventually ground to a halt after the hotel changed hands, and things fell into disarray. When the previous operators, who still owned the property, took it back, they reopened the bar but didn't bring the brewery back to life. In 2008, the property changed hands. During the next few years, Vance Hinton and investor Mike Crowe added a much-needed infusion of capital to remodel the hotel while keeping its turn-of-the-century charm and bringing back the restaurant and bar before giving serious attention to the brewery.

Ray Mittleldorf—who had seen the closure of Two Rows Brewing, Houston's only brewpub at the time, while he was head brewer—was brought on as a consultant to Faust and given the resources he needed to bring the brewery up to snuff. When the system issues that had plagued past brewers had been fixed, Mitteldorf was asked to stay on as head brewer; he now makes Faust Golden Ale, Vinny's ESB, Altered States Altbier, Mike Crow IPA and—because about every old hotel in Texas claims to be haunted—Walter's Ghostly Pale Ale, named for the friendly ghost that has been spotted on the premises. Seasonals include Dullahan Stout, Hell Fire Irish Red, Octoberfaust Märzen lager and Ray's Damnation Barleywine.

Mitteldorf said, "I'm primarily a traditionalist. That's what I like to make, and that's what I like to drink." But he still occasionally enjoys experimenting with other ingredients to make crowd pleasers like Orange Honey Wheat or aging some of the higher-alcohol brews in used bourbon barrels for those who want a rare treat.

The brewing side has taken advantage of its relationship with Chef Chris Kilisz to put on a Brewmaster's Dinner series featuring wild game and food pairings. The kitchen also has incorporated the house beer into some of its signature dishes, including the beer cheese soup and a beer cheese sauce for both the German nachos and the pastry-encrusted bratwurst dubbed Faust Wellington.

With the ebb and flow of brewers opening and closing across the state, it may have seemed a gamble when Keith Moore opened Dodging Duck Brewhaus in a small town away from the bright lights of San Antonio. But Moore, who moved to Boerne after working in Europe in brewing equipment sales, thought that the timing was right with a growing residential base and a steady stream of adult tourists with a taste for good food and local beer.

The Dodging Duck opened on August 1, 2002, with a name inspired by the large number of ducks that sometimes bring traffic on River Road to a halt on their trek between the area around the pub to Cibolo Creek.

Ray Mitteldorf, who had been at the late Houston Brewery and Yellow Rose, was the first brewer at Dodging Duck and used his and Moore's recipes to make numerous beers with duck-themed names. From 2002 to 2005, Dodging Duck won three gold and three silver medals in the World Beer Championships, an international competition.

After Mitteldorf's return to Houston, Moore took the brewing reins and continues to put out four to five house brews at a time on his ten-barrel system in a building adjacent to the main restaurant. The lineup of as many as twenty different styles each year includes clever ducky names such as Sir Francis Drake Porter, Lonesome Duck Pale Ale, Quackinator Doppelbock, Ducktoberfest, Darkwing Dunkelweizen, Fowl Play IPA and Wary Widgeon Wheat Ale.

This period of rediscovery of beer variety and local brewing roots in San Antonio also included the startup beer marketing organization Alamo Beer Company. Eugene Simor, a transplant from California with real estate interests in San Antonio, decided to sell a beer using the city's most enduring symbol. In 2003, he paid Real Ale Brewing Company in Blanco to make a refreshing ale for him under the name Alamo Golden Ale. For seven years, he self-distributed bottles and kegs throughout the area in the back of a minivan before signing with a distributor. The dream was always to open his own brewery in San Antonio, but that would take eleven years to become a reality.

Chapter 8

Resurgence

2008-2013

For San Antonio brewing, 2008 was a pivotal year. A new brewery hadn't opened in the area since 2002. Since 1994, three brewpubs opened and closed, the Faust was in flux and awaiting rebirth and the two defunct microbreweries were becoming distant memories. Even the venerable Lone Star Brewery had closed in 1996. Pearl Brewery brewed its last batch in 2001. Only Blue Star in San Antonio's Southtown and Boerne's Dodging Duck remained.

In March of that year, the *San Antonio Express-News* proclaimed, "Remember 2008. The year that marks the 75th anniversary of the repeal of Prohibition also could bring the biggest expansion of the craft beer movement Texas has seen since it began to crawl up from the devolution left by the alcohol ban." After the failures of the last local beer boom, that was less than certain, but it proved prophetic.

What the city lacked in local beer it was making up for in greater access to and interest in something that had gained the moniker "craft beer." The Flying Saucer Draught Emporium added a San Antonio location in 2000, stores such as H-E-B's Central Market and Whole Foods carried more beer variety from all over the country and the beer selection at the stalwart Hills & Dales (a beer bar before it was cool) gained a greater following.

It was in this environment that economist Scott Metzger moved back to San Antonio after a stint as a bank examiner at the U.S. Treasury Department in Dallas and into a job at the Fortune 500 company Valero Energy Corp. He chose an apartment complex next door to the Flying Saucer, with its eighty taps and more than one hundred bottles, to engage in a regimen of nightly research. Metzger said that the inspiration came to him while on a ski trip to New Mexico in early 2006, when he was surrounded by great beer made in the area, friends and not enough oxygen.

Freetail Brewing Company, a brewpub with sandwiches and just-right pizzas from a brick oven, opened in a fast-growing part of San Antonio with few residents who were likely to travel downtown or to Boerne for fresh beer. The brewery is named after the Freetail Mexican bat native to the area, and the brewery participates in preservation efforts for winged creatures losing ground to breakneck residential development.

The official opening day was Black Friday 2008, the day after Thanksgiving. There were chamber of commerce members, financial institution executives, investors, family and media on hand for the ribbon cutting. The only thing missing was Freetail beer. Problems with the boiler had delayed the brewing process, and it wasn't until late in the year that patrons had their first taste of the house brew.

Metzger hired Jason Davis as head brewer for the new pub. Davis served as assistant brewer to Joey Villarreal at Blue Star before joining Freetail. He also did a short stint as the last brewer at the Laboratory Brewing Company. Before making his way home to San Antonio, he cut his teeth as a brewer at Austin's Waterloo Brewing Company, the state's first brewpub, and at the

Freetail Brewing Company's original location on the North Side has delighted patrons since 2008 with an eclectic selection of beers and pizzas from a brick oven. *brewstravelers365.com.*

Celis Brewing Company, founded by legendary Belgian brewer Pierre Celis. John Lee, also a former Blue Star brewer, later joined the Freetail team as assistant brewer before it opened.

It wasn't just the scarcity of breweries in San Antonio that got people talking when Freetail opened but also the nature of the beer. There were conventional classics like pale ale, La Rubia blonde ale and the signature first beer, a malty and hoppy American amber called Freetail Ale (now known as Freetail Original). But beyond that were twists on the classics, like brewing a classic Belgian witbier with the addition of 15 percent rye malt to make the Rye Wit. Turning styles on their heads or just designing a great beer regardless of style was the defining operating procedure for the brewers. "We're trying to defy—or at least not worry about—style," Metzger said when the brewery introduced its first batches at the end of 2008. "If a beer works in a style, then that's great, but who needs guidelines?"

Although Freetail went through a massive growth spurt starting in late 2014, the original brewpub location at Loop 1604 and Northwest Military Drive still serves as a hub of innovation for the brewing staff. Experimental IPAs share tap tower space with more traditional versions. Interesting ingredients such as prickly pear cactus fruit, cocoa nibs and roasted chiles find their way into small batches. Other early seasonal beers that still emerge in Freetail's lineup are the Belgian golden strong ale ThreeTail and the powerful malt master Old Bat Rastard. And longtime customers still shoulder their way in every November 1 for a taste of cult favorite La Muerta, a stiffly alcoholic and luxurious imperial stout released every year on the traditional Dia de los Muertos, or Day of the Dead.

The buzz created after only a year of being in business, along with the unavailability of the beer outside the brewpub, made it one of the most talked-about new breweries in Texas. While not as rare now that Freetail has a bottling line, special bottle release days still can draw hundreds of people from all over the state.

It also served as inspiration for the next wave of brewers to make the leap of opening a brewery in San Antonio. Despite a burgeoning new beer scene, Metzger was once asked how he might respond to those who say that they do not enjoy a fine brew. He replied, "They just haven't met a beer they like yet." Words to live by, one might say.

What was still missing in San Antonio was a microbrewery. In Texas, brewpubs could sell their beer for on-site consumption or takeaway only in bottles or growlers. Beer producers with a microbrewery license couldn't sell

The windmill at Ranger Creek Brewing and Distilling welcomes visitors to the state's only combined brewery and distillery—or, as the guys like to call it, the only "brewstillery." *Jeremy Banas.*

at the brewery, which made for eventful free beer parties during a brewery open house, but they could self-distribute or hire a distributor to get the beer into bars, stores and restaurants.

Three friends with day jobs at the San Antonio–based insurance giant USAA and a beer industry veteran acting as head brewer stepped in to fill that void. Not only was Ranger Creek Brewing & Distilling Company the first microbrewery in San Antonio in a decade, but it also had bragging rights to being the first brewery with a distillery in the state.

Mark McDavid, T.J. Miller and Dennis Rylander took their love of beer and food into their business plan, which was to make great beer and keep in mind both how it drinks by itself and when paired with food. That philosophy has made Ranger Creek a popular restaurant partner for beer dinners throughout the region. The founding brewer at Ranger Creek, Rob Landerman, developed his love for beer and food while working at the Flying Saucer Draught Emporium locations in San Antonio and Austin. It drove him to get his Cicerone certification, a designation that shows a command of all things beer, including identifying off flavors in beer and their causes, beer and food pairing, brewing and draft systems.

By September 2010, Ranger Creek was producing four beers from its Northeast Side location on Whirlwind Drive, including an oatmeal pale ale (OPA); South Texas Lager; Mesquite Smoked Porter, with malt smoked in a converted shipping container in back of the brewery; and a Belgian dark strong ale dubbed La Bestia Amiable. While Landerman took care of the beer, Miller headed up the distilling side of the operation, but it would be more than four years before Ranger Creek would release beer aged in its own used bourbon barrels.

After five years in business, several of Ranger Creek's original beers have gone into the recipe archives and numerous new beers were created, including the eclectic numbered Small Batch series, with delights such as English-style barley wine, blackberry sour and imperial sweet potato stout. Landerman moved to Boise, Idaho, to launch his own brewery, but under brewer Holland Lawrence, the brewery has refined its Strawberry Milk Stout seasonal with fresh Poteet strawberries and introduced new year-round brews like the Red Headed Stranger Red IPA, Purple Rhine Berliner Weisse and black IPA Dark Side of the Hop.

One successful new brewpub and one successful microbrewery were bound to beget more breweries as homebrewers and craft beer lovers saw the possibilities. In December 2012, Corpus Christi native Jason Ard and his wife, Laura, declared Branchline Brewing Company officially open. Head brewer William Les Locke worked with Ard to scale up the homebrewer's recipes and started making Shady Oak Blonde, Evil Owl Amber and Woodcutter Rye IPA for draft accounts around the city.

The ten-barrel brewery with several twenty-barrel fermentation tanks got its railroad-themed name from Ard's memory of listening at night to whistles and clatter of boxcars from the trains that passed his grandfather's South Texas farm on two railroad branchlines off the main line.

Besides serving as a tribute to his late grandfather, Ard said that the name "holds a lot of meaning in what we are trying to do with our beer, branching out of our three main styles to create some pretty amazing beers. It also stays in tune with our history and story of how we came to start the brewery."

Branchline's recognizable logo greets local residents as they come in for a pint during one of the brewery's open houses. The railroad-themed logo honors owner Jason Ard's grandfather and the trains that he heard at his grandfather's home as a child. *Jeremy Banas.*

All shiny and ready to go, the taps in Branchline Brewing's taproom serve up hand-crafted local love at special events. In the background can be seen one of the brewery's fermentation tanks. *Jeremy Banas.*

A glass of Rye IPA adorns the bar in Branchline Brewing Company's taproom. *Adam Barhan.*

Branchline started strong with special releases and seasonal beers created by Locke. Many of those same beers are still in the lineup, even as new head brewer Paul Ford has been adding to the legacy with new beers from the Northeast Side brewery, near the busy intersection of Thousand Oaks Drive and Wetmore Road. Those beers include 5 AM to Midnight, White Cap Coconut Cream Ale and Menger 32 Pumpkin Ale. "We want to have beers everyone will enjoy," Ard said. That includes the more esoteric brews from the barrel-aging program, which features limited releases that take as long as a year to mature and gain character from the wood.

The beers are now available on draft and in cans, with some releases in twenty-two-ounce bottles after nearly two years of building its draft accounts. "Cans just make sense in Texas and are definitely better for the beer," Ard said.

The craft beer train didn't stop with Branchline in 2012. Newspapers and blogs began routinely reporting on brewpubs, microbreweries and new craft beer establishments under consideration.

The Granary 'Cue & Brew was the first to grab on to one of the oldest pieces of San Antonio's brewing history and opened in the former Pearl

Brewing complex in November 2012. In this case, the brewery and chef-driven barbecue restaurant found a home in the one-time residence of Ernest Charles Mueller, who arrived from Germany in 1890 to take over as chief cooper at the Pearl Brewery. Mueller was brought to Texas by his friend and former Anheuser-Busch co-worker Ignatz Hrovat, then brewmaster at the Pearl. The Mueller house was the central meeting place for the family, and it stayed in the Mueller family until 2004, when it was sold to the Pearl complex.

The brothers behind the Granary are Alex and Tim Rattray, who set out to bring back to the Pearl locally made beer more than a decade after the historic brewery ceased operations for good after 115 years in business. The Granary became part of the massive effort to revitalize the old brewery area into an in-vogue shopping and dining area in San Antonio. Heading up the kitchen is Tim Rattray, who is no stranger to restaurants. He was involved in opening Pearl restaurant originals Il Sogno and the Sandbar. Alex, who gained a love of beer after spending time in England, began homebrewing years ago and set out to master his craft before opening the brewpub. Alex took classes from the respected Seibel Institute of Brewing in Chicago to help gain production brewing experience.

After pitching their idea for a brewpub to the Pearl Brewery LLC, the Rattray brothers were shown several properties as possible locations.

Residing in the former house of the Pearl's original cooper, the Granary 'Cue and Brew was the first to restart the brewing tradition at the Pearl when it opened in 2012. *Jeremy Banas.*

They eventually settled on the Mueller house, not knowing at the time the location's historical connection. Even with an expansion of the building to include space for the massive smoking pit, things are tight in the old house. A seven-barrel brewhouse with several fermentation and serving tanks takes up space, but not so much that they didn't also cram in a good number of guest taps from other Texas breweries, including cask-conditioned ales served with two old-school beer engines. The brothers plan to open a second, larger location in the coming years. Regular house brews on tap year round include the Rye Saison, IPA and Brown Ale.

On the food side, the brewpub serves traditional barbecue fare with counter service available, as well as your meat by the pound. Come back in the evening and you'll find a more full-service approach, with waitstaff, food pairings and a more relaxed feel, with barbecue styles from around the world. Why the different approaches? Tim said that they wanted to make lunch efficient and accessible for those on the go but have a relaxed, elegant option for the dinner crowd.

Both the beer and the 'cue are all artisan in approach, the Rattrays said, with a focus on getting as many local ingredients as possible. The meat is sourced from ranches that humanely raise their animals, something Tim said has become a passion of his in recent years. The brothers approach the brewpub in the best way, taking care of their customers and employees and only sourcing ingredients from those who have the same philosophy. A blog post on the brewpub's website in 2012 summed up this philosophy: "We are a globally inspired barbecue restaurant, rooted in Southern hospitality, hand-crafting our own beer."

The year 2012 also brought a microbrewery to New Braunfels in the form of Guadalupe Brewing Company, named for the river that runs 230 miles from Kerr County, through New Braunfels and into the Gulf of Mexico. Owned and operated by Keith and Anna Kilker, Guadalupe Brewing officially opened its doors in May 2012 and quickly gained a reputation for quality beer. The brewery focuses distribution in the New Braunfels area, Austin and San Antonio.

"I traveled all over the world and had gained a love of many [beer] styles," Keith Kilker said. "I wanted to bring that to Texas." That kindled a desire to brew the same flavorful beers he had found in his travels. He took classes from the Siebel Institute of Technology, which included an internship with Tom Hennessey of Colorado Boy Pub & Brewery in Ridgway, Colorado.

Armed with newly acquired brewers training, Keith and Anna Kilker wrangled the financing, an industrial location on the edge of New Braunfels and an efficient ten-barrel brewing system with economy in mind. Keith Kilker's experience as a controls engineer came in handy when converting and integrating used dairy equipment into the brewing process. A one-time dairy homogenizer serves as the mash tun, with the addition of custom-fitted false bottom and sparge arm, and a converted milk tank does duty as the hot liquor tank.

Keith and Anna have several year-round brews, with special and seasonal releases to keep things interesting. Guadalupe's core lineup includes the flagship Texas Honey Ale, Rye IPA, Scotch Ale, Americano Wheat and Chocolate Stout. "We want to make drinkable beers," Keith said. "We want to keep things simple in our approach to how and what we brew." Both Keith and Anna had visited several breweries in the Pacific Northwest and had what they describe as a "religious beer experience" in the tasting and the inspiration brewers are willing to give one another. He said that he believes it's the craft brewing industry's collaborative qualities that are making it such

Guadalupe Brewing owners Keith and Anna Kilker taking a break from the heat with brewer Jason Barrier and enjoying one of their own malted concoctions. *Jeremy Banas.*

a powerful force in the beer world. "We have to be evangelical in our support of craft beer." They also are evangelical in their support of local ingredients when available, such as buying red winter wheat used in the Americano from farmers in the New Braunfels area and sourcing the honey from Austin. A portion of proceeds from the IPA go to support the sustainability of Big Bend National Park, and some honey ale proceeds—thanks to Anna's involvement as a member of the Alamo Bee Keepers Association—go to support the preservation of honey bees.

The Kilkers say that they don't want to overdo things when considering their growth. "It's all about knowing where you can go and growing organically," Keith said. They have taken over several spaces connected to the brewery for production expansion and a bigger taproom.

Although New Braunfels Brewing Company officially opened in 2010, it counts May 2013 as its date of rebirth in the heart of New Braunfels, taking its name from the city's last brewery before Prohibition. Owners Kelly and Lindsey Meyer had a bit of a false start with hard-to-manage equipment and a run of bad luck in the brewery. Rather than back off and find the path of least resistance, the couple shut down the brewery, sold their chain of fitness centers and went, as they say, "all in."

Outfitted with a bigger and better brewing system and more production know-how than the previous outing, New Braunfels Brewing Company has gained more taps in bars throughout the region and produces a wide selection of bottled beers, including special releases.

The brewery has stuck to its guns in staying with an 85 percent wheat malt in many of its signature beers, including its hefeweizen Luftweiss. The heavily wheat-based lineup of beers also includes the dark Erdeweiss, the hop-forward Feuerweiss, a light and tart lemongrass-infused Wasserweiss and the saison-inspired Himmelweiss. Additions such as coffee, yerba matte and even breakfast cereal transform existing brews into new creations.

New Braunfels Brewing also has done a lot of experimentation with small-batch sour beers bearing names such as Cosmic Dancer, Mexican Cannon, Les Fleurs du Mal, Spread Eagle and Thunder Kiss. The strongest beer in the seasonal offerings is Shiva's Wrath, a cold-lagered and roasty variation on a weizenbock that weighs in at 9 percent alcohol by volume.

Chapter 9

Beer Boom

2013-2015

Compared to the previous decade, five new San Antonio–area breweries in the five years from 2008 to 2012 seemed like a breakneck pace, but 2013 proved to be a watershed year that would break many of the restraints holding back small Texas breweries. The state laws governing breweries, especially those considered microbreweries and brewpubs, hadn't kept up with the times. It had been twenty years since the laws allowing brewpubs passed.

When Texas microbrewers, led by Brock Wagner of Houston's Saint Arnold Brewing Company, asked the Texas legislature for the ability to sell a limited amount of beer to go for visitors in the tasting room, they were sent packing in 2007 and 2009. The powerful and well-funded beer distributor lobby was against the measure, as were big beer companies. Their contributions were no small part of the war chests the lawmakers needed to get reelected.

In 2011, Wagner was back again, this time asking for the right to sell a limited amount of beer to go to those taking a tour of the brewery premises, the way brewpubs could. The new proposal even had the support of the two major lobbying groups for the state's beer distributors. It looked like a done deal, but the support of the former opponents came with the caveat that the large breweries in Texas, namely Miller's brewery in Fort Worth and Anheuser-Busch InBev's plant in Houston, couldn't be part of the deal. Strategically, when it was too late in the session to make changes to the bill, lobbyists for the Belgian beer giant Anheuser-Busch InBev objected to the

ALAMO CITY HISTORY BY THE PINT

proposal because it precluded it from selling beer during its tours. At the time, the company hadn't given public tours of its Houston brewery for fifteen years. The sleight of hand was enough to thwart small breweries from eking out a little more income to support their growth plans.

Also in 2011, other voices emerged. The brewpubs and consumers were asking for updated laws that would allow brewpubs to have the same rights as microbreweries in selling their beer to retailers. This time, the two warring beer distributor lobby groups broke ranks, with the old-line group Wholesale Beer Distributors of Texas against changing the laws and breakaway Beer Alliance of Texas lending public support to the small breweries. Even with just one dissenting voice against those of consumers, small business owners and even other alcoholic beverage interests, the measure never made it out of House committee. Although his arguments were persuasive, bill sponsor State Representative Mike Villarreal of San Antonio was a Democrat bringing a bill to a Republican-dominated committee.

Scott Metzger of San Antonio's Freetail Brewing represented the members of the Texas Craft Brewers Guild and became the name and face tied to the effort, generating enthusiastic press coverage of the issue and making a case for modernizing brewery laws in the state; this would create jobs and bring more revenue to state and local coffers, as well as new opportunities for distributors to diversify their business. So it was Metzger who led the charge again in 2013. It seemed an uphill battle. It was only the second attempt in two sessions to change both the microbrewery and brewpub laws, while it took the Texas wineries ten years and five legislative sessions to bring lawmakers around to letting them sell directly from their tasting rooms. How could beer have it any easier?

But this time was different. Wholesalers had seen the writing on the wall and realized that growing breweries were going to need them for an efficient delivery system. Representatives of both beer wholesaler groups, the Texas Craft Brewers Guild, the giant brewing companies and beer consumer advocacy group Open the Taps crammed in under the bright fluorescent lights of an unused hearing room and put all their cards on the table. At the end of the meeting in the bowels of the Texas capitol, they had all signed an agreement that they would support a slate of beer bills before the Senate Business and Commerce Committee and wouldn't try an end run through another legislator to put in an unacceptable amendment or lobby Governor Rick Perry to veto the measures. After the Republican-authored and bipartisan-sponsored beer bills left the

Marching with purpose, Freetail founder Scott Metzger is flanked by Texas Craft Brewers Guild lobbyists as he heads to the Texas capitol building in Austin in 2013 for the passage of several bills that are transforming Texas brewing. *Sheena Bellavance.*

Senate committee to go to a full Senate vote, Metzger said, "We have a deal signed by all the parties involved. As long as everyone stays true to their word, this will be the law."

On May 21, 2013, the Texas House of Representatives passed the "craft beer bills" sent by the Senate weeks earlier. Senate Bill 515 allowed breweries operating under brewpub licenses to make up to ten thousand barrels of beer per year, double the previous cap. They also were allowed to self-distribute up to one thousand barrels per year if they sold only their products at the brewpub. They are still allowed to carry guest taps and wine alongside their own beer, but they can then only distribute off-site through a licensed wholesaler.

Senate Bill 516 and SB 517 allowed breweries with the microbrewery designation to have an annual production of 125,000 barrels or less and self-distribute up to 40,000 barrels per year with a permit. At the time, only the Spoetzel Brewery of Shiner, Anheuser-Busch InBev and MillerCoors produced more than 125,000 barrels per year in Texas.

SB 518 allowed production breweries with an annual production of 125,000 barrels or less to sell up to 5,000 barrels per year for on-site consumption. This meant microbrewery taprooms could become sources of income, as could anniversary or monthly parties at the brewery. The bill still barred production breweries from selling beer to go to consumers at the brewery for off-site consumption.

The poison pill in the works was SB 639, introduced by the Senator John Corona, chairman of the committee giving all the bills their first hearing. The measure made it legal for a wholesaler to sell its territorial distribution rights from a brewery to another wholesaler. On the flip side, the bill made it explicitly clear that it would be illegal for a brewery to receive compensation from a distributor in exchange for territorial distribution rights, thus putting into law a common practice that had been vague for years. Corona's bill also prohibited a practice called "reach back" pricing, where brewers would charge the wholesalers higher prices for the beer based on how much the wholesaler marked it up to the retailer.

Microbreweries especially weren't crazy about losing their ability to sell distribution rights to wholesalers, even if it may already have been prohibited, because it was money they counted on to expand after years of building their brands in the public consciousness. The bill did still allow, however, for breweries and distributors to pool their money on advertising and promotions around the brands. The microbreweries also were miffed that they wouldn't get the chance to sell beer for takeaway from the brewery, while brewpubs gained the right to sell on-site and to go and distribute. But it was an all-or-nothing deal. If even one bill was voted down, all five would fall.

Ultimately, the new laws led some already established microbreweries to change their licenses to those of brewpubs for more flexibility. Many breweries opened in the San Antonio area after passage of the law opted to start with a brewpub license but cast away the traditional model of serving as a brewery and restaurant. Instead, they can now make maximum profits on their beer at tasting rooms without the staffing issue, overhead and uncertainty of the restaurant business.

Even before the game-changing laws went into effect, 2013 was a time for a slate of new breweries in the area and throughout the state. BS Brewing Company, bearing the initials of owner and brewer Brian Schmoekel, became the first brewery in Guadalupe County since the early 1900s when he put his first beers in bars in June 2013. The brewery put out its College Chronic, a 7.5 percent ABV red ale, and Seguin Ale to favorable reviews and quickly began experimenting on the small-batch brewing system. He says he wants to make beers that people enjoy but also that challenge some of their preconceived notions about what beer should taste like. Those beers can be experienced in bars across the region and on the brewery patio Friday and Saturday evenings, when the brewery welcomes those who make the trek deep into the countryside to enjoy standards and one-off specialty brews.

A pecan ale with honey, featuring local ingredients, was a popular addition to the year-round lineup. Another experimental beer made by BS all year is the strong Pale Reserve, a blend of bourbon barrel–aged Seguin Ale and fresh Seguin Ale that can only be found served on the patio. Caedmon's Ale is a lightly smoked juniper Viking ale with rye, barley, an "antique" German wheat malt—a portion of which is smoked over pecan wood—and two uses of juniper berries from trees found on the ranches around the brewery. The 1888 Whitechapel is a dark English strong ale inspired by Jack the Ripper. Mennonite Pale is a farmhouse pale ale fitting of the brewery's rural locale. And Pungent IPA is brewed just once a year as what Schmoekel calls a "borderline double IPA" weighing in at 8.7 percent ABV.

Shortly after BS began hitting the taps, a second brewery opened in Guadalupe County in the town of Cibolo. From the start, the 5 Stones Artisan Brewery went against the conventional wisdom of brewing what you want

Thirsty patrons of The Cove restaurant line up at the back bar known simply as the Texas Bar, selecting beers from a multitude of taps dedicated to Texas craft beer. *Travis E. Poling.*

but making sure that there are at least a few styles everyone can recognize. Instead, longtime homebrewer Seth Weatherly set up his nanobrewery to make beers full of character and nontraditional seasonal ingredients. "A friend introduced me to homebrewing years ago, and I just fell in love with it, especially the creative aspect of it. I found myself brewing almost every weekend and just couldn't do it enough," Weatherly said.

The signature beer at 5 Stones is the Aloha Piña, a golden ale brewed with copious amounts of fresh pineapple and a healthy dose of roasted local jalapeños. The brew won a bronze medal at the Great American Beer Festival in 2014, garnering even more attention than the three-barrel brewery could handle. An expansion was in the works as of late 2015.

Weatherly took a page from the biblical story of David and Goliath for his brewery's identity. Seeing how competitive the overall beer market had grown, he was in awe of the uphill battle that he and other small breweries now face. "When coming up with a name, David and Goliath stuck with me, and most know David killed Goliath with one stone. But I wondered, how many stones did he actually pick up to take on Goliath? He picked up five," Weatherly said.

The entire beer rotation on shelves, where it is sold in 750mL bottles, is based on the seasons, with four core releases each season. Other beers in 5 Stones' growing portfolio include Rhubarb Cherrylicious wheat ale, Camo pale stout with cocoa nibs and espresso beans, Manmosa wheat ale with fresh pulverized oranges and the spice- and vanilla-laden Merry Christmas ale. Other favorites include the strawberry and vanilla bean blonde ale Norma Jeane; Toby G's, with roasted pecan, vanilla bean and honey; the s'mores-inspired Snipe Hunter; and Flower Child, an amber with chamomile, piloncillo sugar and lemon zest.

The third brewery to make its debut in 2013 was Busted Sandal Brewing Company, located on the edge of the South Texas Medical Center in northwest San Antonio. Co-founded by friends and IT veterans Michael DiCicco and Robert Garza, what began as an idea in 2001 took root a dozen years later. As an environmental responsibility measure, the brewery's all-electric ten-barrel brewhouse includes a tankless flash water heating system, and they use chemicals that are more environmentally friendly for cleaning and sanitizing. Busted Sandal also subscribes to CPS Energy's Windtricity initiative, which brings renewable, wind-powered energy to homes and businesses.

Busted Sandal's name was inspired by a broken sandal that shared a memorable journey with the founders in the formation stages of the

Busted Sandal co-founder and owner Mike DiCicco with Roland Tamez as they prepare for taproom hours. *Busted Sandal.*

brewery. The core beers include Slippery Rock IPA, El Robusto Porter, Fire Pit Wit and 210 Ale. "We would have loved to open with something outrageous, but we want to establish ourselves and our brand before getting too crazy," Garza said. The brewhouse, fermentation and bright tank capacity were all expanded in 2015, and a canning line was installed. The brewery now has distributed outside San Antonio as far away as Houston.

Limited specialty beers at Busted Sandal work off its core brews for creations such as El Gourdo Pumpkin Porter; Headlights IPA, brewed to support breast cancer awareness; and special cask offerings at the taproom like Watermelon 210 Ale.

The fast-paced growth continued in 2014 with three new breweries. They entered a climate unlike those that came before them. Beer bars were popping up even faster than the breweries; growler stations gave people an outlet to take fresh, local beer home; brewery tours and events were drawing hundreds; San Antonio Beer Week had expanded to include several major events; and the fall San Antonio Beer Festival had grown in popularity as more people discovered craft beer and wanted to know more. That eagerness carried over into restaurants and even old-school neighborhood bars looking for a few interesting taps.

It was in this environment that Boerne Brewery opened under head brewer and co-owner Fred Hernandez. Hernandez and his wife, both engineers, designed the brewery while perfecting recipes that honored the area's German brewing roots but added a Texas twist. The six-thousand-square-foot facility broke ground in 2011 on property formerly owned by longtime Boerne residents Edgar and Anna Voges, who had lived in the Boerne area since the early 1900s. Pieces of the original farmstead, like rock from the façade and corrugated metal from nearby sheds, found their way into the brewery design. "This area and this land have a lot of history

Gathered together to brew 2015 San Antonio Beer Week's collaboration beer (a hoppy saison) are representatives from Southerleigh, Alamo Beer, Ranger Creek and Freetail, posing on the steps of Ranger Creek's thirty-barrel brew system. *Top row, left to right*: Josh Kahanek, Nicholas Adcock, Holland Lawrence, Tyler Applegate and Gregg Spickler. *Seated*: Jeremy Banas. *Bottom row, left to right*: Les Locke, Ashley Cooper and Jason Davis. *Kevin Hobbins.*

that we want to honor with our beers and community involvement," said Hernandez, pointing out several Sinclair Oil signs found on the property that now adorn the brewery's walls.

Although the equipment arrived in 2012, it wasn't until the summer of 2013 that they were able to start brewing. Distribution began in January the following year. "Our equipment was manufactured in China," Hernandez said. "Not surprisingly, it was built to design specifications and not standard engineering. The parts are not interchangeable." Once the kinks were worked out, they began brewing four year-round beers. The Denim Hosen starts as a traditional kölsch-style wheat brew but uses a red wheat for that Texas twist while maintaining a crisp finish for Texas summers. Willy's ESB is a hybrid of an extra special bitter and a pale ale, boasting a heavy malt profile but a light mouthfeel. Old Courthouse Ale presents as an English old ale with notes of roasted barley and nuts. Hopstrasse, despite its German-sounding name, is a moderate American IPA that goes for a malt and hop balance.

The logos boast artwork indicative of Boerne's German roots, with each design rendered by area artists. The beer names also tie into the area's history. Willy's ESB is named for one of Boerne's most prominent citizens, William George "Willy" Hughes, a rancher from England who settled in Boerne in 1878. Old Courthouse honors Boerne's center of Kendall County government and the second-oldest courthouse in Texas. Hopstrasse references the town's main street, Haupstrausse (a German term akin to "Main Street"). "We're about community," said Hernandez, who pointed out that the Voges family won a contest to name the town's beer festival Berges Fest, which is held each year on Father's Day.

Seguin Brewing Company was founded by Brian Wallace and Shaun Washington, two graduates of Seguin's Texas Lutheran University. Wallace was a baseball player and later returned to TLU to coach and teach. It was then that he discovered his love of homebrewing. His second batch was the beginning stage of the brewery's signature Honey Pecan Cream Ale using the two ingredients for which Seguin is best known. Washington played football at TLU and entered a career in food and beverage sales after graduation. He brings a business and finance background to the brewery and is the self-proclaimed "Chief of Sampling."

Like BS Brewing, Seguin Brewing is located in a rural area east of Seguin. The tasting room leads out to a sprawling lawn, a shade tree and cable spool tables to while away an afternoon the first Saturday of each month. Found mostly in twenty-two-ounce bottles, other Seguin Brewing beers include the crisp 9-Pin kölsch, Lake Breeze Summer Blonde, Oktoberfest and the strong winter seasonal Black Rye Reserve.

At the end of 2014, Alamo Beer Company, which had been marketing its contract-brewed Alamo Golden Ale for more than a decade, finally cut the ribbon on its own brewery just east of downtown San Antonio. Alamo opened its brewery, large tasting room and beer garden to the public in March on the 179th anniversary of the Battle of the Alamo. Chanting the famous battle cry, "Remember the Alamo," brewery founder and president Eugene Simor not only fulfilled his dream but also brought Alamo beer back to San Antonio. The original Alamo Beer had been brewed by the Alamo Brewing Association not far from the new brewery more than one hundred years earlier.

Simor first conceived Alamo Beer in 1997, and five years later, he introduced the beer made for him at Real Ale Brewing. After growing popular in the local San Antonio area, Alamo Golden Ale quickly expanded to West Texas, South Texas, Houston and Austin.

Building the new brewery wasn't without challenges, as it sat near a politically charged landmark. Simor owned the lot next to the historic Hays Street Bridge, which had been restored with money raised by volunteers and some grants as a walking and biking route that picturesquely linked the East Side to downtown. He also struck a deal with the city to buy donated land on the other side of the bridge to build the brewery and make the lot he already owned into parking that wouldn't block the view of the downtown skyline from the bridge. Arguing that the land was supposed to be a park, people involved in the bridge restoration fought back, eventually taking the city to court. With numerous delays and no resolution in sight, Simor built the sprawling brewery on his original lot but didn't build it as close to the bridge or as high as he had originally planned.

With backing from District 2 councilwoman Ivy Taylor and then San Antonio mayor Julian Castro, Alamo Beer received a unanimous vote from the city council to proceed with construction of the roughly eighteen-thousand-square-foot brewery that includes three separate structures: the brewery and bottling building, the beer hall and an administration building. The Germany-meets-Texas beer garden is surrounded by the buildings. High glass windows facing the beer garden and the bridge highlight the gleaming brewing equipment inside.

Under brewmaster James Hudec, the beers coming from the brewery still include the familiar Alamo Golden Ale, while an amber lager, a German pale ale using German hops and a classic German pilsner have joined the regular

Alamo Beer head brewer James Hudec, who got his start in brewing in Austin in the early 1990s, was classically trained in Germany as a brewer. *Alamo Beer Company.*

lineup. Seasonal beers like maibock and hefeweizen fly quickly from the tasting room during its evening hours Thursday through Saturday. Design of the brewery complex was given to local design firm Lake|Flato Architects, which was also instrumental in the recent restoration of the Pearl Brewery complex.

"This has been a struggle for over a decade. The benefits to the surrounding community are huge," Simor said of his dismay at opposition from the Hays Street Bridge Restoration Group as well as a handful of local residents and some cyclists who have had no qualms about drinking free beer on the vacant lot each year during San Antonio Beer Week. "We plan to incorporate specific areas for cyclists," he said. While the brewery is not currently tied directly to the bridge, he believes that it would help revitalize and draw people to the area. The local beer-to-go bar Big Hops Growler Station recently opened a location at the foot of the bridge and has quickly turned into a laid-back nightspot for Dignowity Hill and adjoining neighborhoods.

None of that has stopped Simor, chief operating officer Jim Walter, chief financial officer John Crider and head brewer James Hudec from making it a focal point of the near East Side and a household name in Texas beer.

Hudec has brewed across Texas, several U.S. states and Germany in his brewing career. "I'm ready to bring classic brewing techniques to the Alamo City," Hudec said over a pint. The brewer got his start helping out at the long-defunct Hill Country Brewing Company while attending Southwestern University in Georgetown, Texas. After his graduation in 1996, Hudec headed to Nuremberg, Germany, and the Neumarkter Lammsbräu Brewery, where he caught the bug for brewing various styles of lagers alongside fellow American Dennis Wehrmann, now of Franconia Brewing in McKinney, Texas. After a few years across the pond, Hudec's career brought him back to Texas, where he became the brewmaster of Two Rows Brewing. By 2000,

Glistening equipment greets visitors to Alamo Beer Company; many pieces of the brewing equipment were modeled on old-world German brewing techniques. *Jeremy Banas*.

he had set out on his own and opened Brenham Brewing Company with his brother. When that venture closed, he traveled and did some consulting for several breweries.

While working on a consulting project for a brewery in Costa Rica, Hudec was enticed back to full-time brewing by Rahr & Sons Brewing owner Fritz Rahr in Fort Worth, but he eventually found himself called to help restore New Orleans' Crescent City Brewing after Hurricane Katrina devastated the city. Hudec was instrumental as a consultant and lead brewer, helping the brewery get back on its feet. He recalled the travel to get to New Orleans: "We had to snake around the river just to get around the military presence. With all the chaos, I kept a .45 at my hip." One year later, he joined Gordon Biersch Brewing in New Orleans as the head brewer, later transferring to the chain's Kansas City location, where he spent five years, before hearing a call to return to Texas. Here was the chance to make the classic German styles he loves, from schwarzbier to Bamberger smoked lagers. "I believe in the traditional lagers of Germany," Hudec said. "So what if they're served with a view of downtown San Antonio?"

By the fall of 2014, the new brewery laws had born fruit when Freetail Brewing Company opened its production brewery on South Presa Street in the

Above: Director of brewing operations Jason Davis with assistant brewers Zach Wolfe and Raimey Roberts bottling up Freetail goodness. *Jeremy Banas.*

Right: Cans of Freetail's Bat Out of Helles helles-style lager prepare to be filled on the brewery's canning line from Wild Goose Canning of Boulder, Colorado. *Nan Palmero.*

former Mission Restaurant Supply warehouse. Thanks to the law that owner Metzger spearheaded, he was able to team up with mega-distributor Silver Eagle to get Freetail beer on shelves and taps from San Antonio to Houston while still operating under a brewpub license, selling beer to go and to drink on site at both the restaurant and large brewery locations. Joey Villarreal of Blue Star didn't need to build a new brewery because he had excess brewing capacity at the original pub and had already started distributing bars in the downtown almost immediately after the governor signed the bill in 2013. Faust Brewing Company is building a production brewery likely to open in early 2016 in a converted Quonset hut and neighboring house just down the street from the hotel, restaurant and original brewery. Other brewpubs were expected to follow suit.

The ultimate merger of San Antonio's brewing history, Texas culinary traditions and the recent reform in the brewery laws happened in April 2015 with the opening of Southerleigh Fine Food & Brewery. The project put a brewery inside the ornate and sturdy Pearl brewing building for the first time since the brewing stopped there fourteen years earlier.

Chef/owner Jeff Balfour (formerly of Citrus at the Valencia Hotel) and head brewer William Les Locke (late of Branchline Brewing) are working

Freetail founder Scott Metzger waxes poetic with visitors on a tour of his new production facility in San Antonio's South Presa area. The new location is dedicated solely to distribution of its beers, a taproom…and a little disc golf. *Jeremy Banas.*

Silence sets over the Freetail brewhouse, creating an unusual sense of calm in the otherwise bustling building. Very soon the smell of good things to come will arrive. *Jeremy Banas*.

in a space that pays homage to the Pearl's past while looking forward to the future and their own identity. Balfour had been looking to open a restaurant with a brewery long before contacting the Pearl management group in 2011, and he thought that the original brewhouse building was optimal. "When you look at the space and the artists' renderings, it's just perfect," Balfour said. "The Pearl group had always wanted brewing to return to the brewhouse." With this revitalization of brewing tradition, both Balfour and Locke hope that it serves as a model for other defunct regional breweries. "We're excited to continue the Pearl tradition with Southerleigh," Locke said. "It's a feeling that can't be put into words."

Southerleigh's building incorporates touches of the much larger Pearl brewery, with remnants of some of the old brewing equipment providing a façade for the modern serving tanks on the mezzanine level overlooking the dining room. The building's original arches also are intact, along with some old pumps and firkins. The brewpub's north wall features an artist's rendering of the original brewhouse blueprints, while the hallway that connects the restaurant and brewery to the Hotel Emma bears an illustrated timeline of the building's history on one wall and house-made beer aging in rum, tequila, bourbon and wine barrels on the opposite wall for special limited releases.

Located off South Presa on the south end of San Antonio's downtown, "Freetail 2," as it's known to locals, houses the brewery's production operations. *Jeremy Banas.*

Dozens of barrels adorn the taproom of Freetail's production facility. Each barrel is filled with various styles aging for future release. *Jeremy Banas.*

Southerleigh features a menu that adjusts with the season, reflecting Balfour's upbringing on the Gulf Coast in Galveston and Houston with a southern comfort food twist. Staples on the menu include hand-rolled pretzels, Texas Longhorn jerky, wood-fired meats, traditional shellfish boils, beer-braised meat and cornbread.

This creativity and innovation doesn't just extend to the food side of the house. Balfour said that he and Locke have an open collaboration with the food and beer menus. "We will be constantly working to create beers that have our dishes in mind and vice versa," Balfour said. Locke also sees a symbiotic relationship with Balfour and the food side of the business. Locke has been known to use unusual ingredients in his beers that can easily pair with almost any dish. "I was excited for the building and equipment to be completed so that Jeff and I could begin working together," Locke said. "He has the same philosophy as I do when it comes to food, and with the unlimited versatility of beer, the pairings will be endless."

Southerleigh usually has ten to twelve house beers available, as well as several guest taps. Regular offerings include the Texas Uncommon (a twist on the California common style with the addition of fresh mint in the brew), a Dortmunder-style lager and the Darwinian IPA, which will be ever-changing thanks to the yeast strains. The six-person brewing crew seems to be having a good time of it when naming the multitude of different beers they are producing, including Putin's Revenge, Dog Ate My Alarm and Soul Redemption. A barrel-aging program will include sour ales as well.

Taking advantage of the new laws, Southerleigh had cemented a deal with distributor GLI to get its beer to select draft, including several bars and restaurants in the Pearl development by the fall of 2015; also, a limited number of bottles were being readied for distribution to stores on a small hand-operated bottling line. Even with a fifteen-barrel system from Portland Kettle Works, demand could outstrip ability to expand within a few years and necessitate Southerleigh following other brewpubs with a freestanding production brewery.

"It's important to us that all aspects of the restaurant and brewery reflect an American feel—specifically southern," Locke said. "We want our customer to feel that they can relate to us when they are here," Locke added. "We want all aspects of the restaurant to be approachable so that regardless of your income level, you'll feel at home here." What's more, Locke wants the servers to be knowledgeable about the house beers and the diversity of beer in general. "We plan to have all servers obtain the Certified Beer Server designation from the Cicerone Certification Program," Locke said.

The small town of Boerne, still enjoying having two breweries to call its own, gained its third in 2015 in the form of Kinematic Brewing Company. The small, family-owned brewery had been in the planning stages for a few years and then had a quiet opening in the summer. Founded by David Fuentes and Jon Beaumont, Kinematic operates a four-barrel brewing system to produce Umbra Imperial Porter, Meridian Belgian Wit, Ascension Double IPA and Declination Pale Ale. The duo is self-distributing in kegs and bottles.

Because they opened with a brewpub license, they also are selling their beer at the brewery for Boerne residents and visitors to drink there or take some home. Beaumont serves as the head brewer and has scaled-up recipes that were part of his homebrewing experimentation. The brewery is using a homebrew-size five-gallon system for experimental and seasonal beers available for sale only at the pub. The taproom opened in late August and is open Saturday and Sunday afternoons, with the occasional food truck on hand.

Mad Pecker Brewing Company, a brewpub years in the making, opened in the summer of 2015 on San Antonio's far northwest side, filling a void of craft beer in that part of the city. Owners Jason and Erika Gonzales raised their startup capital the hard way: they saved it. "We saved a lot of our own money for years," said Jason. "We were able to buy our property, kitchen equipment and brewing equipment without taking out a loan."

The brewpub on Tezel Road just north of Culebra Road is in a former pizza joint that the Gonzaleses completely refurbished with help from friends. Jason, like so many brewery owners before him, started out homebrewing and waiting for a chance to open his own place. Mad Pecker started off with a one-barrel system, the smallest in the city, but that makes it a struggle to keep

Mad Pecker Brewing Company's steampunk-inspired feel is represented in its logo, as well as on the mural that adorns the kitchen, designed by local artist Mike Arguello. *Jeremy Banas.*

six to eight of its beers on tap. The two have already started saving for a larger brewing system even as they enjoy being a small brewery serving their neighborhood.

Still to come in 2016 is OK Brewery and Eishaus, which has found a space in San Antonio's Hemisfair Plaza downtown and not far from the iconic Tower of the Americas. The park, originally built to hold the numerous structures and exhibits of the 1968 World's Fair, is undergoing a complete redo, and the brewpub figured into those plans.

The small brewpub headed by Vera and Brent Dekard will have gastropub takes on traditional German fare. Although they are still doing test batches on different styles, the brewery promises to use locally sourced ingredients when possible and always keep one of two "easy drinkers" on tap.

Another brewing venture poised to open its own brewery in San Antonio is Naughty Brewing Company, from James Vaello. He now works with Adelbert's Brewing in Austin to produce the signature beers, which have been on the market since November 2013. The name came from a comment by his wife, Kathryn, after he started homebrewing again. "I got Katie drinking craft soon after. First time I brewed, she took a sip and said, 'Oh honey, that's naughty.' It's just kinda stuck," Vaello said.

With plenty of seating and locally inspired cuisine, visitors to the Friendly Spot receive a hearty dose of the local, Texas and U.S. craft beer selections. *Jeremy Banas*.

Sporting a wide variety of U.S. craft beer, Big Hops places a large focus on Texas breweries at its three San Antonio locations, which also specialize in growler fills. *Jeremy Banas.*

Big Hops' original location opened in February 2013 and has since added two more locations. *Jeremy Banas.*

At Adelbert's, he makes Naughty's I Think She Hung the Moon, a dark saison with notes of spice, hibiscus and smoke; and Zijden Kousen, a Belgian-style IPA with notes of citrus, pine and a sweet malt backbone. Although these first two offerings were Belgian in nature, Vaello later introduced a variety of other styles, including Kentucky Streetwalker, an imperial vanilla porter aged in Four Roses bourbon barrels.

While on a tour of the Adelbert's brewery, Vaello struck up a conversation with Adelbert's co-founder Scott Hovey, and the two hit it off. "I'd expressed my desire to Scott that I was looking to open my own place," Vaello said. What resulted was Vaello licensing the image, name and recipes for Naughty Brewing to Adelbert's, which handles the production. Vaello then represents the brands in the markets across the state. "My wife and I are thrilled to be able to get our ales out on the shelves," said Vaello, who hopes to be able to break ground on his own production facility in San Antonio within a few years. "We want to get a good sales history behind us first," he said, "then we'll see where we're at."

Two of the smallest towns to have breweries are Spring Branch and La Vernia. The Shade Tree Saloon and Grill quietly makes beer in-house and sells it to customers as "homebrew." It's a long-popular Spring Branch hangout for everyone from area ranchers to motorcycle enthusiasts traveling U.S. Highway 281 between San Antonio and Blanco, but it was a surprising place to find an unadvertised brewpub. In La Vernia, population 1,034, Donny's Brew Pub has been licensed by the state to brew and was remodeling an existing building for the new venture in August 2015.

The San Antonio area is rich in a history of brewing that many would like to see preserved. While the beers made as they were before Prohibition are gone, the buildings of the once great breweries in the city are finding new life, sometimes even with brewers providing a pulse to the long-empty hulks. But San Antonio also is writing a new history in beer that could rival, or at least keep pace with, the proud Austin beer scene. One clear difference between the brewing tradition of old San Antonio and today is that breweries are supporting one another instead of duking it out with promotions and ad campaigns to capture the hearts and minds of the public. Instead, brewers are creating a new tradition of visiting one another's taprooms, exchanging ideas, giving advice to the new kids on the block, collaborating on special beers and even sharing ingredients in a pinch.

It's unlikely that we'll ever see a new brewery smokestack reach into the sky or the ornate brewery architecture once in fashion, but the legacy of the new breed of San Antonio brewing could last even longer than bricks and mortar. These times will be remembered in the beer we drank and the people we drank it with.

Breweries Around San Antonio and Brewing Resources

MICROBREWERIES AND BREWPUBS

Because operating hours, tour times, dates tasting room hours and even locations can change, please use the brewery websites to plan your trip before you visit. This list includes all brewpubs and microbreweries in Bexar, Comal, Guadalupe, Kendall, Wilson and Atascosa Counties as of August 2015, including several undergoing construction at the time.

ALAMO BEER COMPANY
202 Lamar Street
San Antonio, TX 78202
alamobeer.com

BLUE STAR BREWING COMPANY
1414 South Alamo, #105
San Antonio, TX 78210
(210) 212-5506
bluestarbrewing.com

BOERNE BREWERY
9 Hill View Lane
Boerne, TX 78006
(830) 331-8798
boernebrewery.com

BRANCHLINE BREWING COMPANY
3633 Metro Parkway
San Antonio, TX 78247
branchlinebrewing.com

BS BREWING COMPANY
1408 Old Lehmann Road
Seguin, TX 78155
(830) 660-8124
bsbrewingtx.com

BUSTED SANDAL BREWING COMPANY
7114 Oaklawn Drive
San Antonio, TX 78229
(210) 872-1486
bustedsandalbrewing.com

Appendix A

THE DODGING DUCK BREWHAUS
402 River Road
Boerne, TX 78006
(830) 248-3825
dodgingduck.com

DONNY'S BREW PUB
198 Farm-to-Market Road 1346
La Vernia, TX
facebook.com/donnysbrewpub

THE FAUST HOTEL AND BREWERY
240 South Seguin Avenue
New Braunfels, TX 78130
(830) 625-7791
fausthotel.com and faustbrewing.com

5 STONES ARTISAN BREWERY
850 Schneider
Cibolo, TX 78108
5stonesbrew.com

FREETAIL BREWING COMPANY
Freetail North Brewpub Location
4035 North Loop 1604 West, #105
San Antonio, TX 78257
(210) 395-4974
freetailbrewing.com

FREETAIL DOWNTOWN PRODUCTION
BREWERY
2000 South Presa
San Antonio, TX 78210
(210) 625-6000
freetailbrewing.com

THE GRANARY 'CUE & BREW
602 Avenue A
San Antonio, TX 78215
(210) 228-0124
thegranarysa.com

GUADALUPE BREWING COMPANY
1580 Wald Road
New Braunfels, TX 781320
guadalupebrew.com

KINEMATIC BREWING COMPANY
635 Highway 46 East
Boerne, TX 78006
kinematicbrewingco.com

MAD PECKER BREWING COMPANY
6025 Tezel Road
San Antonio, TX 78250
(210) 562-3059
madpeckerbrewing.com

NEW BRAUNFELS BREWING COMPANY
180 W Mill Street
New Braunfels, TX 78130
(830) 626-2739
nbbrewing.com

OK BREWERY AND EISHAUS
560 South Alamo
San Antonio, TX 78210
(210) 861-4852
sabrewingco.com

RANGER CREEK BREWING AND
DISTILLING
4834 Whirlwind Drive
San Antonio, TX 78217
(210) 775-2099
drinkrangercreek.com

SEGUIN BREWING COMPANY
320 Beiker Road
Seguin, TX 78155
seguinbrewing.com

SHADE TREE SALOON & GRILL
13430 Highway 281 North
Spring Branch, TX 78070
(830) 885-5550
theshadetreesaloonandgrill.com

SOUTHERLEIGH FINE FOOD &
BREWERY
136 East Grayson Street, Suite 120
San Antonio, TX 78215
(210) 455-5701
southerleigh.com

BREWING CLUBS

BEXAR BREWERS
bexarbrewers.org

This group holds meetings and beer-style exploration sessions monthly and puts on the annual Alamo City Cerveza Fest, a statewide homebrew competition that is part of the Lone Star circuit.

SAN ANTONIO CERVECEROS
sanantoniocerveceros.org

A community of craft-beer enthusiasts organized to educate the public about the enjoyment of craft beer and homebrewing. Major events include Brews & Blooms with the San Antonio Botanical Garden in May, Learn to Homebrew Day in November and participation in San Antonio Beer Week's Golden Age of Homebrew each spring.

HOMEBREW STORES

HOME BREW PARTY (NORTHEAST SAN ANTONIO)
15150 Nacogdoches Road, Suite 130
San Antonio, TX 78247
(210) 650-9070
homebrewparty.com

Appendix A

Home Brew Party (northwest San Antonio)
8407 Bandera Road, Suite 103
San Antonio, TX 78250
(210) 520-2282

Gabriel's Liquor & Wine Superstore (far north central San Antonio)
1309 North Loop 1604 West, #109
San Antonio, TX 78248
(210) 492-8585
gabrielsliquor.com

San Antonio Homebrew Supply (near downtown)
111 Kings Court
San Antonio, TX 78212
(210) 737-6604

Re-creating Charles Degen's "Famous Beer"

It bugged me while researching this book that there was no information anywhere on the recipe that Charles Degen used to brew his widely popular beer—the very beer the *United States Health Bulletin* deemed the purest beer in the United States in 1902. Yes, Degen was well known not to have shared the recipe or even talk about it, but I just couldn't accept that.

As discussed in the second chapter, a ledger of the Menger Hotel gave us a few clues about the recipe and the beer itself. Although we do not know what style of beer he brewed, we do know that his beer was known to be very strong, hence the building of the hotel to accommodate patrons who would sleep overnight. Considering that this was the mid-nineteenth century to early twentieth century when Degen was brewing, we know that most ales and lagers of that time in the United States were more seasonable. The ABV (or alcohol by volume) was at or below 5 percent, allowing a consumer to have more than one. So, to say that Degen's beer was stronger likely puts it anywhere around 6 percent ABV or higher, making it is possible that Degen altered the style he was brewing to meet his wants.

We also know that the Menger Hotel ordered Blaffer malts. Research into this malt showed that this was not a malt varietal at all; instead, it refers to a brewing supplier out of New Orleans by the name of J.A. Blaffer & Company. Ship manifests of that time indicate that Blaffer & Company received its shipments from St. Louis, Missouri, and Cincinnati, Ohio. This makes sense, considering that both American cities were major brewing centers at the time and both were home to domestic maltsters. There's no mention, of course, of the type of malt ordered; however, if we take into account the malt used in the United States, even by German immigrants, the less refined six-row malt is our likely suspect. Like many things over time, some malts are popular but then disappear as new, more popular ones are created. "At least in North America, barley is continually tweaked by selective breeding programs, and 'very solid players' have their years in the sun, then fade away," said Jaime Jurado, director of brewing operations for Louisiana's Abita Brewing Company, an industry veteran and previously a longtime San Antonio brewing executive. Discussions with Sabine Weyermann, president of Weyermann Malt, founded in 1879 in Bamberg, Germany, narrowed the closest equivalent available now to Weyermann Bohemian Floor Malted Pilsner. This varietal is floor-malted in the same way malt would have been in Degen's time.

Although the 1850s did not see the same, more refined two-row malt varietals that we enjoy today, some two-row malt varietals were available in the United States. Around the mid-nineteenth century, the few German ales—Altbiers and Kölsch specifically—that were being brewed (lagers were more popular) were using German Pilsner malt (also referred to as German Two-Row). Since Degen's beer was also known to have been a little darker than the lagers of Germany, it's likely that specialty malts such as Caramel or Munich were also used. The altbier style has its origins in the city of Dusseldorf, as well as northern Germany, and is typically fermented slightly colder than other ales and then lagered (cold-aged) for smooth lager characteristics and seems to be our likeliest suspect in terms of the style Degen brewed, especially since his beer was aged in the cool underground tunnels.

We know also that Degen used one local ingredient: piloncillo sugar, native to South Texas and Mexico. The use of this sugar during the brewing process easily could have amped up the ABV, but it would also have given the brew notes of molasses, a flavor common in this type of sugar.

We know from the Menger Hotel ledger that Irish and California hops were ordered. No mention is made of the varietal of the hops from Ireland. Considering that hops are not native to Ireland, we can rule that out, although hops from England were usually brought in. The ledger also indicates that he paid for Guiterman Spalt. Degen may have purchased German Spalt hops (Spalter Hops in today's brewing world), which originate in Spalt, Germany, and still could have been purchased via Ireland.

Some varietals of hops were native to the United States at that time, such as Cluster hops (a cross breed of native hops and those brought over from England) and *Humulus lupulus neomexicanus*. However, it is more likely that Cluster hops were used.

As for the yeast, there is no mention of what Degen used. If we are to surmise that it was indeed an altbier, we are down to two likely candidates:

a German ale or kölsch yeast from the Cologne region of Germany and Düsseldorf alt yeast from, you guessed it, Düsseldorf, Germany. Accounts in the *San Antonio Light* at the time describe Degen's beer as being on the bitter side, to which the German ale/kölsch yeast is better suited.

So here we have it: the closest approximation to Degen's original recipe we are likely to get.

GRAIN
8 pounds Weyermann Floor Malted Pilsner Malt 2.5L
2 pounds Caramel 60L
.75 pound Munich Dark 20L

HOPS
1 ounce Cluster hops at 60 minutes
1 ounce Spalter hops at 20 minutes

YEAST
White Labs WLP 029

ADJUNCTS
16 ounces piloncillo sugar at 30 minutes

Pre-boil: 1.049
OG: 1.061
FG: 1.015
ABV: 6.1 percent

Efficiency: 77 percent
32 IBUs

Mash in at 152 degrees for 60 minutes. Boil should be around 90 minutes to help reduce DMS (an off flavor that tastes like cooked corn). Pre-boil volume should be adjusted to allow for the longer boil. Cool and then rack into a primary fermenter and ferment between 64 and 69 degrees. Once fermentation is complete, move into a secondary vessel and lager (cold age) between 35 and 40 degrees for 4 weeks.

—Jeremy Banas

Notes on Recipe Formulation

All this talk of beer throughout the book might have you wanting to try your hand at brewing. Whether you are new to brewing or more experienced, creating your own recipes can be very rewarding. Maybe you've gathered the equipment needed and some books and even talked to veteran brewers. You might even have many partial mash or all-grain batches under your belt. But perhaps something is missing. While you are enjoying the brewing process, getting to know your equipment and honing your techniques, gaining more control over the process can be more of a challenge.

I confess that I probably brewed at least four or five all-grain batches before I finally felt ready to try my hand at creating my own recipes. I was scared to death. Trying someone else's proven recipe is safe, and if you make a mistake or two, it's likely to be close enough. Working on your own recipe puts the added stress of not getting the recipe right and making a move that can make or break your beer, even on a perfect brew day.

There are dozens of books out there that will assist with recipe formulation and getting to know everything that needs to be considered. However, there are a few in particular that I keep close at hand: Ray Daniel's *Designing Great Beers*, Randy Mosher's *Radical Brewing* and the recently published *Brewing Better Beer* from Gordon Strong. I suggest looking at these and any others as your resources.

So, where to begin? You first have to decide what you want your beer to be, starting with the style. From there, you need to decide what character your beer will have. If it's a porter, will it have more chocolate flavors or do you desire more roast character? How hoppy do you want your beer? Does the malt character you're looking for fit the style, or do you plan to deviate a bit?

The next step is to determine your grain bill, as well as your mash technique. This is the basis for the character of your beer and determines your total fermentables. These days, most malts are heavily modified, so you will be able to use a single-infusion mash at a temperature usually between 148 and 154 degrees Fahrenheit depending on style. I say this because each grain produces a different amount of fermentables, and the temperature used affects the body of your beer and how much sugar you get from it, which also can affect your yeast attenuation down the road. As such, you will need to consider the fermentables produced by each malt and how they work together to help you decide what base malt you will use and what specialty malts are needed.

Almost as important is your water profile and the amount of water needed. The minerals in the water can add a very distinct flavor to your beer. You'll want to find out the profile of your local water, what minerals are in the style you are brewing and what will be needed to treat your water. I've gone back and forth on this issue, and I know many brewers who have as well. If you're wanting to brew an exact clone of your favorite beer or match the water to the style, then duplicating the brewing conditions, including the water profile of the area where that beer is brewed, will be important. Although I have treated my water a few times, most often I used the local water untreated (mixed with an even amount of reverse osmosis water) for my brewing. Using the untreated water in my area is what helps make my beer *mine*.

You've decided what you want to brew, selected your grains and thought about your water. Now comes the time to decide what flavor and aromas you want in your beer and the IBUs (International Bitterness Units). You have a few choices. You can set your IBUs to style or set them based on what you are looking for. Ask yourself if you want more aroma, more bitterness or a balance between the bitterness and the aroma. Take into account your grain bill as well and make sure the hops don't overpower your malt (unless you're brewing a double IPA, then it's game on).

It's been said by many that the yeast chosen is what truly defines your beer's identity. Yeast is your beer's soul. You can brew two batches with the same grain bill, water and hops, but if you use different yeast for each batch, you'll get two similar but very different beers. I've brewed a black saison and a rye IPA several times with different yeasts, and they have turned out great but very different. Choosing yeast for the style you're brewing and what flavors you're looking for is important. You'll need to take into account the OG (original gravity) of your beer and estimate what your target FG (final gravity) will be to ensure that the yeast chosen has an attenuation that suits this.

After your yeast has been chosen, take into consideration what you'll use as a fermentation vessel. Will you use an airlock or blowoff tube? What's the temperature you'll need to maintain, and how will you control it?

Lastly, look at how you'll clarify and carbonate your beer. To clarify your beer, there are several ways to accomplish this, Irish moss and Worflock tablets being two. Clarifying your beer can be very important if you're entering your homebrew in a competition, but just for yourself, that's up to you.

Once your beer is ready, you have two decisions as to how you want to disperse and carbonate it: kegging or bottling. For many new homebrewers, bottling is the easiest and least expensive. You need only to calculate the proper sugar/water mixtures based on your volume of beer and the style so as to reach the appropriate level of carbonation; you also need a bottling bucket and wand. Another benefit of bottling is that if you plan to gift some of your homebrew or send it to a friend, you already have a vessel for this. Bottling can be tedious, often taking several weeks to fully carbonate, and it often made me dread the process.

Kegging your beer has its pros and cons as well. However, in my opinion, the cons appear in the beginning. To keg, you'll need to buy a keg, CO_2 tank and CO_2. The cost can be around $200 to start, but once these are purchased it's only a matter of refilling your CO_2 tank. The cost to refill a standard 5- to 7.5-gallon tank is about $20, and it can last several months.

After you've purchased these items, simply rack the beer from the fermenter to the keg, shake it around a bit and hook up the CO_2. Set your CO_2 to about 25 psi for a few days, and at that point, the beer should have absorbed plenty of the CO_2. You can dial it down to about 10 psi for everyday serving. This method gets you enjoying your beer sooner.

That's it in a nutshell. As I was working on a recipe for a pumpkin porter, I really got to thinking about my approach to formulation and how much I enjoy tinkering with a recipe. This certainly isn't all-encompassing, nor is it meant to be, but it can serve as a guide to formulating your own recipes and perhaps even dabbling in re-creating your own historic brew from what clues you can find.

—Jeremy Banas

Bibliography

Bechtol, Ron. "Heads Up for San Antonio Suds." *San Antonio Light*, April 4, 1985.

———. "Just Brew It: Local Pubs Tapping into National Trend." *San Antonio Express-News*, n.d.

Bexar Archives. "Diego de Santos' Certification on Taxes on Aguardiente and Wine Transported from Laredo to Bexar." Dolph Briscoe Center for American History at the University of Texas–Austin, document dated June 11, 1774.

Carroll, Bess. "Where Foaming Mead Once Flowed." *San Antonio Light*, May 31, 1929.

Cox, Wayne. "Brewing: A Bubbly Catalyst." *San Antonio Express*, January 15, 1966.

Daniels, Ray. *Designing Great Beers.* Boulder, CO: Brewers Publications, 1998.

Goff, Myra Lee Adams. "Phoenix Saloon Applies for Historical Designation." "Around the Sophienburg," July 27, 2014. sophienburg.com.

Gonzales, Teresa. "Comprehensive History of the Menger Hotel." Methods of Historical Research class, Dr. Albro, University of Texas at San Antonio. Part of a term paper given to the Daughters of the Republic of Texas Research Library.

Haas, Oscar. *The History of New Braunfels and Comal County.* Austin, TX: Steck Publishing Company, 1968.

Hennech, Michael C., and Tracé Etienne-Gray. "Brewing Industry." Handbook of Texas Online. Texas State Historical Association. http://www.tshaonline.org/handbook/online/articles/dib01.

Hillert, Patricia. "Brewmaster Brings S.A. Fame." *San Antonio Light*, May 15, 1949.

Hix, Martha Rand. "They Made It a Pearl: Pearl Brewing Company's Managers during Its First Three Eras (1886–1943)." A work privately prepared for the owners of the former Pearl Brewery complex, June 2004.

Holley, Joe. "Pearl Story Is Saga of 3 Emma's." *Houston Chronicle*, November, 28, 2014.

Mosebach, Fred. "Early Breweries Tell Interesting Story of Beer that Made San Antonio Famous." *San Antonio Light*, August 25, 1935.

New Braunfels Herald. "Staunch Civic Leader Caught in Brisk Anti-Slavery Conflict." *Braunfels Herald*, May 9, 1961, 6A.

Old Breweries Information. oldbreweries.com.

Poling, Travis E. "Mugs Runneth Over." *San Antonio Express-News*, March 26, 2008.

———. "X." *San Antonio Express-News*, January 7, 2009.

Ramsdell, Josephine. "Old Menger Bar Plans Move." *San Antonio Sunday Light*, March 11, 1945.

Rhodes, Andy. "Brewing Heritage: Texas' German Immigrants Hoisted History with Old World Traditions." *Medallion* (Fall 2013). Texas Historical Commission.

San Antonio Light. "For 50 Years Charles Degen Has Brewed a Famous Drink." November 21, 1909.

———. January 20, 1980.

———. "'Underground' of Past Years Is Forgotten." *San Antonio Light*, September 11, 1938.

Sophienburg Museum & Archives. "Julius Rennert Brewery." Pages copied from a larger, typewritten and unidentified work and placed in the Rennert family files.

Strong, Gordon. *Brewing Better Beer*. Boulder, CO: Brewers Publications, 2011.

Texas Reader. "The First Texas Brewery." www.texasreader.com/the-first-texas-brewery.html.

Ulrich, Kristi M., Barbara Meissner and Maria Watson Pfeiffer. "Archaeological Monitoring of the Urban Reach Section of the San Antonio River Improvement Project, San Antonio, Bexar County, Texas." Archaeological survey report no. 407. University of Texas at San Antonio, UTSA Libraries Digital Collections, 2009.

Valentine, Maggie. *John H. Kampmann, Master Builder: San Antonio's German Influence in the 19th Century*. New York: Beaufort Books, 2014.

Wolford, Sam. "Menger Was Oasis." *San Antonio Light*, February 15, 1959, and February 22, 1959.

Index